# LOSE IT *for*
# LIFE®
## *for Teens*

# LOSE IT *for* LIFE®

## *for Teens*

The Spiritual, Emotional,
and Physical Solution

## Stephen Arterburn, M. Ed.
## Ginger Garrett

INTEGRITY®
PUBLISHERS
family

*Nashville*

LOSE IT FOR LIFE for TEENS

Published by Integrity Publishers, a division of Integrity Media, Inc.,
5250 Virginia Way, Suite 110, Brentwood, TN 37027.

HELPING PEOPLE WORLDWIDE EXPERIENCE *the* MANIFEST PRESENCE *of* GOD.

Stephen Arterburn and Ginger Garrett published in association with Alive
Communications, 7680 Goddard Street, Suite 200, Colorado Springs, Colorado 80920.

Cover Design: Brand Navigation, LLC (Bill Chiaravalle, DeAnna Pierce, Terra
              Petersen)
Cover Image: Iconica/Laureen Middley
Interior: Inside Out Design & Typesetting

Library of Congress Cataloging-in-Publication Data

Lose it for life for teens : the spiritual, emotional, and physical solution / Stephen
  Arterburn and Ginger Garrett—[2nd ed.].
        p. cm.
  Summary: "Focuses on finding and maintaining correct weight for life for teens.
Dealing with why they overeat and helping set good habits for future"—
Provided by publisher.
  Includes bibliographical references.
  ISBN 1-59145-248-1 (tradepaper)
1. Weight loss. I. Garrett, Ginger, 1968– II. Title.
  RM222.2.A783   2005
  613.2'5'0835–dc22                                              2004026732

*Printed in the United States of America*
05  06  07  08  09   DELTA  9  8  7  6  5  4  3  2  1

*To you, my reader and friend.*

*May the seeds of hope root deeply in your soul,*

*and may you blossom always with your face towards the Son.*

# CONTENTS

# Who's Talking?

## A Message from Steve & Ginger

*Steve Arterburn*

Hi, I'm Steve Arterburn, the founder of Lose It For Life. I know what it's like to feel like you are in a race you'll never win with your weight. I've struggled with my weight too. That's how I began to discover the keys that can unlock the prison of being overweight. I combined these keys to freedom into this program called Lose It For Life. I wanted to develop a program that would provide the motivation and inspiration for gradual weight loss: doing it the right way, with the right frame of mind.

In fact, I co-wrote a book for adults based on this program called *Lose It for Life.* (If your parents struggle with their weight too, this would be a great book for them to read.) But as much experience as I've had with my program, leading over one thousand people into discovering how to lose weight for life, I've never had the experience of being a teen girl. So I asked my friend Ginger Garrett to help me translate the principles of this program into a book that young women will relate to.

**Ginger Garrett**

I'll tell you my story later, but you need to know I'm the one talking in the book. So when you read stories about squeezing into girdles, that's me talking. (Oh, how I wish I hadn't admitted quite so much to you in this book!) Steve's expertise—and what makes this program so powerful—is in giving you all the keys to freedom, not just one. His experience has taught him that lifelong weight loss is a combination of the spirit, heart, mind, and body. But he doesn't have any experience wearing a bikini, or striking supermodel poses, so he had to rely on my experience in those departments. So although I'll be talking directly to you in this book, it's Steve's wisdom and experience, and his materials from the Lose It For Life seminars, that made this book possible. Just to be sure you're not confused when you read the book, let's try a pop quiz:

*Who wears the Manolo Blahniks in this book?*
   a. Ginger
   b. Steve

*Who created Lose It For Life?*
   a. Ginger
   b. Steve

*Who does most of the talking?*
   a. Ginger
   b. Steve

*Who is the true genius*
   a. Ginger
   b. Steve

**Answer Key:**
1. a     2. b     3. a     4. That depends on whose mother you ask.

# A PERSONAL NOTE

Hi! My name is Ginger, and I wrote this book for you. I've been praying since before it was even published that God would use this message to impact your life—and that you would journey with me on this road to freedom.

You probably want to know if I've ever struggled with my own weight. Well, I wouldn't use the word "struggle" to describe my journey . . . no, what I went through could more correctly be termed a knockdown, dragged out, full-blown war. I've encased myself into girdles so rigid I couldn't even raise my voice for fear my rubber dam would burst. I've squeezed myself into pants so tight that if I ever blew a seam, someone would have lost an eye. I've railed at God for cursing me with hippo hips and thunder thighs even as I inhaled a box of chocolates. When my scale read highest, my spirits hit the depths. But I've also known extreme thinness and the euphoria of winning the diet war. *Temporarily.*

Many summers ago, I was thin. Really thin. My bones stuck out at all angles and my bra fit better backwards. The only problem was, although my scale said I was thin, I didn't feel thin. I didn't think I looked thin, either. I certainly didn't wake up euphoric and walk around all day to appreciative stares. Nope, it was just me, smaller but no taller. But I remember clearly the day I quit dieting forever. After a dinner date with my boyfriend, a competitive athlete and stickler about weight (mine, that is), I came home, kicked off my shoes, and climbed up on my kitchen table with an entire ice cream pie and a spoon. Sitting Indian-style, I made up for all the food I had denied myself, and while I did so I wondered what to do with my life.

You see, I had learned that struggling to maintain a too-thin body was just as hard as trying to lose weight. And the harder I tried to find happiness through my weight, the more miserable I became. So in between bites of fudge and ice cream, I assessed my lifestyle and my love life. By morning, both the pie and the boyfriend were history. Along with them, I gave up the dream of being perfect. I thought this also meant I had to give up the idea of being loved and accepted, because without dieting, I would never be as perfect looking as the models on TV. Yet it was too exhausting to keep trying and always fall short of my goal, so I just decided to give up and fall short forever.

**THE REALITY? I HAD TO LEARN HOW TO LIVE WITH FOOD AND ACCEPT MY IMPERFECTIONS.**

But with that decision, I wasn't free . . . and I wasn't happy. For years, the only way I knew to deal with food was to eat everything in sight that I craved and then get back on my diet. I lived every day believing I was either crawling towards thinness or rolling down the hill of obesity, which is sort of like a snowball getting bigger with every revolution.

The reality? I had to learn how to live with food and accept my imperfections.

So I started a project. I decided to read every verse in the Bible about food, weight, and appearance. I wanted to know everything God had ever said on the subject. And as I read, a new vision for my life came into my heart and mind. I began to understand that God didn't value thinness the way I did. God wanted to give me so much *more* than a good weight.

Then I met Steve Arterburn, the man who founded Lose It For Life. The principles he teaches in his Lose It For Life seminar really lined up well with what I had read in the Bible. There was a good balance between grace and discipline. When he asked me to write this book for teens, I was ecstatic. If he had been in the room, I would have knocked him over as I rushed to my computer!

So here we sit—I, typing these words on a rainy afternoon, and you, reading this book and wondering if this book will really work . . . if you really *can* lose it for life. Well, I think you can. I did. If you've struggled with your weight, been hurt and humiliated by mean remarks and embarrassing situations, thought that a perfect body would change everything, then we have plenty in common! And because you're reading this book, we're going to have even more in common. I am now at a healthy weight, and someday soon you will be too—because you are now reading this book.

Being overweight can feel like being locked in a prison. The keys to unlock that prison are in your hands, and this book will show you how to use them. Sometimes we want God to instantly cure us, to work a miracle by giving us a perfect body and taking away our bad habits. Yet God doesn't seem to be in the business of zapping people into shape. The real miracle you're going to experience in Lose It For Life *is not about the numbers on the scale.* It's the healing that will take place in your spirit, heart, and mind. Along the way you will discover why you eat and how you should take care of yourself each and every day.

The goal isn't to lose weight, because most people can do that, but to *lose weight for life.* The secret isn't dieting, which is why so many other books have failed at this effort. Instead, this book brings new hope because the focus is on living, not dieting.

In fact, one of the best experiences you'll have on this journey is the realization that God created food for your pleasure and good health. He intends for you to eat several times a day and enjoy delicious foods that taste great and give your body energy and strength. Food was created to be a blessing, a constant reminder that God's blessings are with us. You won't find endless lists of bad foods versus good foods, or be asked to eat foods only in weird combinations or at certain times of the day. *Lose It for Life for Teens* will change much more than what you weigh or eat—it is *life-changing*.

God wants to lead you into a new life where you know how deeply loved, cherished, and accepted you are. In the end, you'll be more slender, though not perfect, and that reality will be okay with you. Remember, I'm praying for you. I want you to begin, even at this very moment, to feel like this book, me, and everything we're about to discuss together creates a safe haven of acceptance and support. *Because you're going to make it. And it's going to be awesome.*

Your sister in the struggle,

# GETTING STARTED

Picture yourself at a party. You're feeling self-conscious about your weight and appearance. After scoping all the other girls out, you conclude you're the biggest one in the room. A couple of guys laugh as you walk by, and you just want to run and hide. There's a bunch of teens outside playing in the pool, but there's *no way* you'd put a bathing suit on in front of this crowd. You pick at the buffet table, trying to act like you hardly ever eat anything. You leave the party early, go home, and pig out.

Have you ever wished for a touch from God—a miracle—that would transform you from an ugly duckling into a beautiful swan? (I have too!) Guess what? In 2 Corinthians 5:17 we are told that when we know Him, our lives *are* transformed: "Therefore, if anyone is in Christ, he is a new creation; the old has gone, the new has come!" Such words should give us great hope for this journey, because a relationship with God is the foundation for losing the weight for life. With this relationship there is support, encouragement, and resolution.

If you're reading this book, you've probably struggled with your weight for a long time. You probably don't feel beautiful . . . or transformed. You may feel ashamed, lonely, desperate. You want so badly to have everyone in the room at that party see how lovely you truly are. You can even imagine the looks on everyone's faces if they could just see how beautiful you are beneath the surface of extra weight and insecurity. What people see on the outside is *not* the real you.

## ARE YOU READY TO BEGIN YOUR TRANSFORMATION?

Are you ready to begin your transformation? If you are, turn the page.

# one

# THE GOAL

Separating Fashion and Feelings From Good Health

## OUR CRAZY CULTURE

A friend of mine, who is about five foot two and 110 pounds, was mad at her doctor. He wouldn't prescribe the latest weight loss drug for her. So she strapped heavy leg weights on her ankles, put on some long, baggy pants, and went to a different doctor with the hope he would think she was overweight and give her the drug. I couldn't understand why she wanted to even try this new drug. Consider these side effects listed inside the package of the most popular weight loss drug currently on the market:

Changes may include gas with oily discharge, an increased number of bowel movements, an urgent need to have them, and an inability to control them, particularly after meals containing higher amounts of fat than are recommended.[1]

I don't know about you, but control of my bowel movements is pretty important. And gas with oily discharge? You might lose weight, but good luck getting a date! Why would anyone be so eager to take a pill with side effects like that? One reason is that we live in a culture that's obsessed with overeating *and* dieting. We're either on our way to an all-you-can-eat buffet (and having second helpings of everything) or buying a new diet book and struggling to chew some celery. In fact, if you went to the mall and looked around, the majority of adults present would tell you they are trying to lose weight—but *after* they finish that chili cheese dog and extra-large soda!

> **WE LIVE IN A CULTURE THAT'S OBSESSED WITH OVEREATING AND DIETING.**

It's been said that if you want to get rich in America, invent a new way to lose weight. *Billions* of dollars are spent every year on diet books, pills, and countless weight loss gimmicks. One diet suggests we can lose weight if we learn to breathe differently. Another tells us we have to eat according to our blood type, and yet another diet says we have to eat to balance the acidity in our bodies. True story: My uncle was convinced he'd stumbled onto the perfect diet plan when he lost forty pounds eating nothing but Cheetos all day. (He also turned orange!) And a famous actress just announced that she lost weight on a diet based on your facial features—apparently, people with big pores will lose weight if they eat oatmeal!

Low fat, low carb, and low sugar are the buzz phrases of our food labels. There are lotions and creams, special sweatsuits, and dental retainers that force you to take smaller bites. My personal favorite gimmick is a special shampoo that readjusts the magnetism of your head. According to the manufacturer, our heads have become de-magnetized, but using this special shampoo will restore the correct charge to your head. *Voilà!* Problem solved. (I just can't bring myself to try the free sample I have. I mean, if a magnet can erase a computer's hard disk, who knows what this shampoo might do to my brain?)

But despite all those billions of dollars being spent to lose weight, Americans are getting bigger:

▼ Nearly two-thirds of adults in the United States are overweight, and 30.5 percent of that group are obese, according to data from the 1999-2000 National Health and Nutrition Examination Survey (NHANES).[2]

▼ The prevalence [toward this trend] has steadily increased over the years among both genders, all ages, all racial/ethnic groups, all educational levels, and all smoking levels.[3]

▼ The percentage of children who are defined as overweight has doubled since the early 1970s.[4]

▼ The percentage of overweight teens has tripled.[5]

Being overweight as a teen can have a devastating impact on your health long-term:

▼ Being obese at age twenty could lop a whopping twenty years off your life.[6]

▼ Today's teenagers may be the first generation of Americans whose life expectancy is shorter than that of their parents.[7]

▼ Obesity is associated with cardiovascular disease, menstrual difficulties, sleep apnea, respiratory problems, type 2 diabetes, psychological disorders such as high blood pressure, gallstones, urinary incontinence (leaking urine accidentally), and more.

▼ Being overweight is closely related to experiencing low self-esteem, depression, and anxiety.[8]

▼ Overweight teens are more likely to become overweight adults.[9]

This is comforting news in the sense that you are not the only one who struggles with their weight. Most of us in America do, no matter how old or young we are. It's important that you don't beat yourself up for having a weight problem. The odds have been stacked in that direction for a long time. Some of the reasons that directly affect teens include school cafeterias with menus full of junk calories and too much fat and restricted school budgets that force budget cuts in physical education programs. Other reasons are more cultural, such as the ten thousand ads for junk food a person in this country is liable to see in a single year, and the fact that Americans enjoy an abundant food supply and very large portions at every meal.

Our culture is all mixed up when it comes to food and dieting. Explaining the problem has led to a variety of popular myths about why we're overweight—the most common of which is assuming a single thing caused the weight problem, such as:

▼ My mom fed me white bread and pasta all the time.

▼ I have a low metabolism.

▼ I hate to exercise.

▼ It's in my genes—everyone in my family is big.

▼ I have a sweet tooth.

▼ I just don't have enough willpower.

The truth is, no *one* thing is solely responsible for a weight problem. Weight problems are caused—and cured—by a group of behaviors that all impact each other. These behaviors fall into four groups:

1. *Physical.* To work best, the human body needs healthy food and exercise every day. A natural law is that "like always produces like." If we eat junk and don't exercise, we'll crave more junk and more rest. But if we eat healthy foods and exercise, we'll create a desire for these things every day.

2. *Emotional.* Our emotions can feel overwhelming, and we can begin craving food as a way to numb ourselves or vent anger and frustration. Dealing with emotions in a healthy way lessens the need to deal with them with a fork.

3. *Relational.* Relationships are probably the number-one source of stress in our lives! Though we can learn how to eliminate much of the stress, we can't eliminate a lot of the people!

4. *Spiritual.* We all have hungry spirits that need to be filled by God. When we aren't full spiritually, we overeat and never feel satisfied. The spiritual hunger that drives us to the refrigerator can't be satisfied with food. When we get filled every day by spending time with God, we feel a peace in our lives that makes overeating unnecessary.

Perhaps you think you'll solve this weight problem once you're grown up and on your own. It doesn't usually work that way. A new study shows that when young people leave home and build their own lives, their weight often suffers.

The percentage of people who are obese doubles from the teen years to the mid-twenties.[10] Working on this challenge as a teen will save you years of heartache later, which is what *Lose It for Life for Teens* is all about.

Most diets want us to change our eating, and that's why most diets fail. No one simply has an "eating" problem. Overeating is a condition of the heart, spirit, mind, and body, and during this journey each area will get an extreme makeover. But, maybe there is *one* thing that can unlock the doors of permanent weight loss.

## THE SECRET WEAPON

How many times have you beaten yourself up for not having enough willpower? Willpower is all about *forcing* yourself to do the right thing. Willpower is white-knuckling it through the dessert buffet and pizza party (and then going home and wiping out the fridge in a fit of frustration). Willpower is a stiff-necked refusal to listen to what the body is saying, a determination to stick to the plan no matter what happens. That being said, here's the secret weapon: *Permanent weight loss takes willingness, not willpower.*

## PERMANENT WEIGHT LOSS TAKES WILLINGNESS, NOT WILLPOWER.

Remember that old saying, "Where's there's a will, there's a way"? They didn't get it quite right when it comes to the weight loss question. You see, it should be: "Where there's willingness, there's weightlessness." In our context, *weightlessness* means that life is no longer defined by what we weigh. Weightlessness means you get up in the morning and your first two thoughts are *not* "I ate too much last night" and "I'm too fat to wear anything cute." Weightlessness means when you walk into a room, you aren't afraid people are judging you by your size, or laughing behind your back when you leave. It sounds pretty great, right? Now on to defining what gets us there!

*Willingness* is having a soft, easy-to-mold spirit and heart that make you *want* to do the right thing. In the context of weight loss, to be willing means trying new measures and letting go of those which are more bad habits than anything else. It means surrendering control to God and adapting our plans to what He tells us. Most importantly, willingness means we're ready to learn all the lessons God wants to teach us from this battle with the scale, the first of which is usually that we're not to obsess over what the scale says.

## THE DIFFERENCE BETWEEN SURRENDER AND CONTROL[11]

| SURRENDER | CONTROL |
|---|---|
| God is the Master of the universe. | I can master all things. |
| God's perspective is higher than mine. | What I feel is all that is important. |
| My circumstances are part of God's eternal perspective. | If God is God, my circumstances must be changed now. |
| I must allow God's plans to open up before me. | My plans are all that matter. I demand immediate results. |
| I accept life knowing that all things work together for my good. | I blame God when life doesn't go the way I think it should. |

The idea of surrendering doesn't sound like the winning strategy in a battle, does it? But when it comes to the battle for weightlessness, surrendering our control to God is the first step. And really, how successful has it been to try and control your willpower? Have you achieved the results you desire? 'Nuff said!

Though surrender doesn't come to us naturally, or happen automatically, we can make the decision to start surrendering right now! Please pray with me.

*Dear Lord,*

 *I surrender. Please show me who You are and what You desire for my life. Help me believe with my whole heart as this journey begins. I can trust You because Your way is so much better than mine. Help me realize whenever I am trying to control You, so that I can surrender and let You control my life. Fill me with Your love and give me what I need to choose Your way and not mine. Amen.*

## WHERE DO I START?

Once you've decided to surrender, it's time to determine the right weight for your height. This should be an objective measurement that demonstrates a healthy, realistic goal for losing weight. Also, a healthy motivation to lose weight should be reflected in this number. You see, some days you might *feel* fat, even when you are maintaining a normal weight.

Sometimes we confuse these two distinct states. Listen up! Everyone, no matter how little they weigh, has days when they feel fat. However, feelings are fleeting, and certainly they are not to be trusted automatically as fact. Remember, our culture is set up to make you think a normal body isn't good enough. Being skinny will not mean you always feel good about yourself. Everyone struggles to some degree to accept their bodies—even supermodels! It's no accident that the highest concentration of plastic surgeons in this country is in the Hollywood/Beverly Hills area—also home to a large percentage of our country's most "beautiful" people. The surgeons have built a lucrative business helping the beautiful people *feel* more beautiful by constantly tweaking the imperfections only they can see. (This is about as annoying as being in a dressing room and overhearing the girl in the next stall complaining that the size 2 jeans are just a little too baggy in the rear.)

| FEELING FAT | BEING FAT |
|---|---|
| Embarrassed to wear a bathing suit | Embarrassed to wear a bathing suit |
| Feel awkward around opposite sex | Feel awkward around opposite sex |
| Low self-esteem | Low self-esteem |
| Hate my body | Hate my body |
| Can easily participate in physical activities | Can't easily participate in physical activities |
| Easy to find clothes in my size | Hard to find clothes in my size |
| Normal BMI* and weight | High BMI* and weight |
| Low risk of health problems | High risk of health problems |

Sadly, being overweight is a serious reality, not just an emotional insecurity. Besides the health risks associated with being overweight, a recent study suggests that teens who are overweight suffer slightly more depression than a teen with cancer.[12] Being overweight can steal your joy and plunge you into depression and despair. But there is a way out, and this book is your roadmap! Lose It For Life is about freedom! Jesus said: "So if the Son sets you free, you are free through and through" (John 8:35 MSG). The point is, being overweight affects much more than just your outward appearance. Let me restate God's promises here, because our heavenly Father never shortchanges us when we ask Him for what we need.

*For your Father knows what you need before you ask him.*

*—MATTHEW 6:8*

*Now to him who is able to do immeasurably more than all we ask or imagine, according to his power that is at work within us, to him be glory.*

*—EPHESIANS 3:20*

*So I say to you: Ask and it will be given to you; seek and you will find; knock and the door will be opened to you. For everyone who asks receives; he who seeks finds; and to him who knocks, the door will be opened.*

*—LUKE 11:9–10*

So maybe you've been asking for a smaller body, but God led you to this book so He could give you much, much more. Or maybe what you really want is a boyfriend, but God wants to give you a true love. Or maybe you just want the teasing to stop, but God wants to make you the most respected girl in school. The good news is, whatever you've been asking for, it's probably not enough! "I am the Vine, you are the branches. When you're joined with me and I with you, the relation intimate and organic, the harvest is sure to be abundant" (John 15:5 MSG).

Knowing the ideal shape and size for your body can be difficult in the midst of the numerous cultural messages bombarding society today. For instance, if you lived in Europe, you'd be told men like women with a little more "meat on their bones." On one remote tropical island, teens can't attract a male until they're overweight. They sit around and eat and pray that they can get big enough to catch the eye of that special village heartthrob. In some African tribes, big buttocks are prized among women. A comment we would find horrifying, such as "Look at how big your rear is!" would be a highly prized compliment in that society. (And in one particular tribe, big buttocks are prized among *men!* How nice to see the men worried about their rear ends, for once!) So the "perfect" size and shape for the human body is relative, and it will change depending on the cultural perspective, time, and place.

## IN THE BEGINNING

God created women to look quite distinct from men. We have a much higher percentage of body fat, most of which is deposited on our hips, belly, and breasts. In fact, throughout history, the ideal body for a woman has been quite plump by today's standards. Being "skinny" wasn't a good thing! It meant you didn't have enough money for food and couldn't have as many babies as a plump woman could. How our bodies work was more of a mystery than it is now, and so being overweight was associated with good things like fertility and money. Besides that fact, life expectancy was very short. Women were likely to die in childbirth or from disease at a very young age.

A social historian, Joan Jacobs Brumberg, studied diary entries from teen girls from the late 1800s in America and compared them with the diary entries of modern teens. The teens of the Victorian era dreamed of being virtuous, kind, and enlightened—to be so was the epitome of womanhood, or so they thought. Good

## BEING THIN WAS IN!

health was important, but having a great body wasn't. (Remember, they were still wearing those very full dresses that went from neck to floor.) In that era, what they *did* was as important as what they looked like. Brumberg's assessment? "Girls today grow up believing that 'good looks'—rather than 'good works'— are the highest form of female perfection."

At the beginning of the twentieth century, a change began to stir among young American women. For one thing, they were hot. Air conditioning hadn't been invented yet, and these girls were wearing petticoats and corsets and heavy multi-layered dresses, all day, every day. Because they were uncomfortable, they dared to do what no teen had done before: They showed their ankles in public! (Please don't faint from shock.) These crazy young women didn't stop there, however. Suddenly those heavy dresses with all the hip-enhancing petticoats were out, while straight and lean and refreshingly cool dresses were in. The young flappers prior to World War I and into the 1920s were the fashionistas of their time with short hair, straight dresses, and very skinny bodies. Their parents were mortified. These young women were showing their ankles in public—and their calves too! (What would these parents have thought of today's bikinis?)

Suddenly, it was *not* cool to have curves. Big hips and breasts were not the style, and neither were those multilayered petticoats and long dresses. The new fashion called for "straight and skinny." Thousands of women wanted to lose weight and fit into these comfortable, cute little dresses. The first best-selling diet book was published in 1918: *Diet & Health, with Key to Calories.*

Over the next few decades, the fashion trend changed a few more times and even embraced a more rounded body shape for a time. Movie stars like Marilyn Monroe made a curvy body cool again, although minus the heavy dress and petticoats. At that point all the naturally skinny girls tried to gain weight! However, as the 1960s approached, very skinny models like the famous "Twiggy" came into fashion. Again, *being thin was in!* Everyone tried very hard to diet down to the "right" size.

Today, electronically altered images of women's bodies appear in every magazine. Plastic surgery is more common than not, and yet there is a weight problem that cannot be ignored. Judging by the most popular models of today, it appears that the ideal body shape is trim as a board, but with breast implants as big as a Cadillac's airbags. And the moral of the story? We are more concerned with what is *fashionable* for our bodies, not what is *healthiest.*

So if you're unsure what the ideal size, shape, and weight for you really is, you're not alone! People have *always* had different answers for this question. And besides, fashion changes from one generation to the next. Let's forget about being perfect or looking like an airbrushed model in a magazine. Instead, let's focus on being healthy and realistic, because perfection just isn't an option—not even for the "perfect" people. Famous celebrities and models spend thousands of dollars on surgery, and yet they still need to have

These days you only get two kinds of pictures of celebrities— paparazzi pictures or pictures like these which have been highly styled, buffed, trimmed, and altered to make the subject look as good as is humanly possible. We do that for everyone, whether they are a size 6 or a size 12. . . . Practically every photo you see in a magazine will have been digitally altered in this way.[13]

their imperfections airbrushed away when they're posing for a photo shoot!

As a teen facing all these pressures and unrealistic standards, your feelings about your body become the dumping ground for all of your frustrations and anxieties. Somehow, you know you're not going to measure up. You are judged more often by appearance than anything else, right? Though adults are judged by what they do for a living, how much money they make, what car they drive, the house they live in, and their politics, teens may judge themselves, and each other, just by appearance.

Your appearance is like a credit card because it can get you things: acceptance, popularity, friends, boyfriends. It can buy your way out of teasing and loneliness. But when you feel pain, whatever the reason might be, the first guess is almost always linked to appearance. *I must not be pretty enough*, you think, or, *I need to lose weight for him to like me.* And because your appearance is one of the only things you can control in your life right now, you'll be tempted to place too much emphasis on it. Sister, learn to give yourself a break from all that pressure to be perfect! I'm not going to lie . . . having a great body is a fantastic asset to being a teen.

But a great body isn't the same thing as a *healthy* body. And while the standards keep changing and a lot of people disagree on what a great body looks like, nobody is in dispute about how important good health is now and how it positively impacts your future.

> # A GREAT BODY ISN'T THE SAME THING AS A HEALTHY BODY.

The next step? Your body is designed to work its best at a specific weight. Scientists call this your ideal "set point." It's the weight at which all your internal systems can get their jobs done while leaving you feeling terrific. It's the place your body wants to get to and will strive to stay at—so let's find that number!

## THE RIGHT WEIGHT FOR YOU

First, there isn't a magic number that fits every person. We're not going to set a hard and fast goal for how many pounds you should weigh. As one expert states,

> To determine ideal body weight, individuals should not rely solely on a bathroom scale, height-weight tables, or percent body-fat measurements. Sound nutrition and exercise science principles, along with common sense, mandate that individuals should avoid setting "hard and fast" body-weight goals. Rather, they should strive for achieving a level of body

weight that is compatible with a healthy lifestyle (e.g., sensible eating, regular exercise, etc.).[14]

So what we can and will do is get an idea of where you are right now and how far from your ideal set point you might be. The three tools we'll use to do this are a Body Mass Index (BMI), a BMI Percentile Chart, and a BMI/Waist Ratio.

We will consult two BMI charts for teens: one that will show you what your BMI is, and another that will show you how your BMI compares to your peers. This is the tool doctors use to determine if you are overweight. Because weight fluctuates as teens grow, it's important to know what your current BMI is as well as how it compares to other teens.

At the end of Chapter One (page 21) is a special place (for your eyes only!) to record where you are at right now. And though it won't be easy, starting here is the best thing you can do for yourself. It's time to see what the numbers are telling you.

### Step One: Determining Your Body Mass Index (BMI)[15]

The table on the facing page has already done the math and metric conversions. To use this tool, find your height (in inches) in the left-hand column. Move across the row to the number that represents your current weight. Follow that number up its column to see what the BMI is for your current height and weight.

For teens nineteen years of age, as well as adults, the BMI can be used to determine if you are of normal weight by using this table. (If you are not yet nineteen years old, skip ahead to the next step.)

# BODY MASS INDEX (BMI)

| BMI (kg/m$^2$) | 19 | 20 | 21 | 22 | 23 | 24 | 25 | 26 | 27 | 28 | 29 | 30 | 35 | 40 |
|---|---|---|---|---|---|---|---|---|---|---|---|---|---|---|
| Height (inches) | Weight (pounds) | | | | | | | | | | | | | |
| 58 | 91 | 96 | 100 | 105 | 110 | 115 | 119 | 124 | 129 | 134 | 138 | 143 | 167 | 191 |
| 59 | 94 | 99 | 104 | 109 | 114 | 119 | 124 | 128 | 133 | 138 | 143 | 148 | 173 | 198 |
| 60 | 97 | 102 | 107 | 112 | 118 | 123 | 128 | 133 | 138 | 143 | 148 | 153 | 179 | 204 |
| 61 | 100 | 106 | 111 | 116 | 122 | 127 | 132 | 137 | 143 | 148 | 153 | 158 | 185 | 211 |
| 62 | 104 | 109 | 115 | 120 | 126 | 131 | 136 | 142 | 147 | 153 | 158 | 164 | 191 | 218 |
| 63 | 107 | 113 | 118 | 124 | 130 | 135 | 141 | 146 | 152 | 158 | 163 | 169 | 197 | 225 |
| 64 | 110 | 116 | 122 | 128 | 134 | 140 | 145 | 151 | 157 | 163 | 169 | 174 | 204 | 232 |
| 65 | 114 | 120 | 126 | 132 | 138 | 144 | 150 | 156 | 162 | 168 | 174 | 180 | 210 | 240 |
| 66 | 118 | 124 | 130 | 136 | 142 | 148 | 155 | 161 | 167 | 173 | 179 | 186 | 216 | 247 |
| 67 | 121 | 127 | 134 | 140 | 146 | 153 | 159 | 166 | 172 | 178 | 185 | 191 | 223 | 255 |
| 68 | 125 | 131 | 138 | 144 | 151 | 158 | 164 | 171 | 177 | 184 | 190 | 197 | 230 | 262 |
| 69 | 128 | 135 | 142 | 149 | 155 | 162 | 169 | 176 | 182 | 189 | 196 | 203 | 236 | 270 |
| 70 | 132 | 139 | 146 | 153 | 160 | 167 | 174 | 181 | 188 | 195 | 202 | 207 | 243 | 278 |
| 71 | 132 | 139 | 146 | 153 | 160 | 167 | 174 | 181 | 188 | 195 | 202 | 207 | 243 | 278 |
| 72 | 140 | 147 | 154 | 162 | 169 | 177 | 184 | 191 | 199 | 206 | 213 | 221 | 258 | 294 |
| 73 | 144 | 151 | 159 | 166 | 174 | 182 | 189 | 197 | 204 | 212 | 219 | 227 | 265 | 302 |
| 74 | 148 | 155 | 163 | 171 | 179 | 186 | 194 | 202 | 210 | 218 | 225 | 233 | 272 | 311 |
| 75 | 152 | 160 | 168 | 176 | 184 | 192 | 200 | 208 | 216 | 224 | 232 | 240 | 279 | 319 |
| 76 | 156 | 164 | 172 | 180 | 189 | 197 | 205 | 213 | 221 | 230 | 238 | 246 | 287 | 328 |

| BMI | YOUR WEIGHT IS... |
|---|---|
| 18.5 or less | Underweight |
| 18.5–24.9 | Normal |
| 25.0–29.9 | Overweight |
| 30.0–34.9 | Obese |
| 35.0–39.9 | Obese |
| 40 or greater | Extremely Obese |

## Step Two: What Percentile Do You Fall In?[16]

If you are a teen under the age of nineteen, doctors recommend that you look at your BMI as it relates to other teens the same age. If your BMI falls below the 85th percentile, you are not considered at risk for being overweight. If your BMI falls right at the 85th percentile, it means you are bigger than 85 percent of your peers and in danger of being overweight. If your BMI falls in the 95th percentile, you are bigger than 95 percent of your peers and definitely overweight.

| BMI PERCENTILE CHART | | |
|---|---|---|
| Age | 85th Percentile (Danger Zone) | 95th Percentile (Overweight) |
| 14 | 23.4 BMI or above | 27.2 or above |
| 15 | 24 BMI or above | 28 BMI or above |
| 16 | 24.6 BMI or above | 28.8 BMI or above |
| 17 | 25.2 BMI or above | 29.6 BMI or above |
| 18 | 25.6 BMI or above | 30.3 BMI or above |
| 19 | 26.1 BMI or above | 31 BMI or above |

## Step Three: Determining Your Waist Size[17]

Research demonstrates that the health risks for being over-weight are greater for those people who carry their extra weight around their waist, such as teens with an "apple" shaped body type. Use your BMI and your waist measurement to calculate the health risks you face with your weight:

### Am I at Risk?

| BMI | Waist Equal to or Less than 35 Inches | Waist Greater than 35 inches |
| --- | --- | --- |
| 18.5 or less | — | — |
| 18.5–24.9 | — | — |
| 25.0–29.9 | Increased risk | High risk |
| 30.0–34.9 | High risk | Very high risk |
| 35.0–39.9 | Very high risk | Very high risk |
| 40 or greater | Extremely high risk | Extremely high risk |

## Step Four: Set Your Weight Loss Goal

So now you know your BMI, how your BMI relates to your peers, and how high your health risk is. Now it's time to determine how much weight you have to lose by using the first BMI chart in reverse. For example, if you are in the 85th percentile (for instance, you are seventeen years old and have a BMI of 25.2), you can use the chart to find the weight for your height that will get you down to a 24.9 BMI or below. Any weight that allows you to fall below the 85th percentile or to a BMI that is at or below what is appropriate for your age (see BMI Percentile Chart, page 18) is a healthy and good weight for your body.

There's no one number on the scale that's healthiest for the same two people of equal height. Some teens may have more muscle, and some teens may have a smaller body frame. By aiming for a healthy BMI rate, you can focus more on lifestyle changes and less on the scale.

Be reasonable when you set a goal weight for yourself. If you have always been on the heavier end of the weight spectrum, it isn't a good idea to pick a BMI of 18.5 (or less) to get to. Instead, start small and stay consistent. A good way to approach weight loss is to do it in blocks of 10 percent. Say a teen weighs 170 pounds but has determined she needs to weigh between 121 and 159 pounds to have a healthy BMI. Instead of trying to diet down to 121 (a number she can't ever remember seeing on the scale!) she would be better served by trying to lose 10 percent of her current body weight. Here are the calculations to make:

170 x .10 (10 percent) = 17 pounds

170 - 17 = 153 pounds

If this teen lost 10 percent of her current body weight, she would be within healthy limits of the BMI. And because her goal is more realistic—losing 17 pounds as opposed to 49—she is more likely to succeed.

*The Earliest Diet Fad?*

**Munching on the heart of a lion to improve athletic performance!**

# A New Beginning

Today's date: _____

My weight is: _____

My current BMI is: _____

Is my BMI at or
above the 85th percentile? _____

My waist (in inches): _____

My current health risk is: _____

My new weight goal: _____

_____

_____

_____

_____

_____

~

*Lord, thank You for loving me*
*no matter what my weight or BMI.*
*Please guide me as I begin to make*
*the changes necessary for my good health.*
*Help me to avoid unhealthy pressures and*
*to focus instead on Your original, best design*
*for my body. Help me to trust You with*
*the final outcome.*

# two

# LET'S EAT!

Feeding Your Body for Lasting Weight Loss

## THE NEW YEAR'S RESOLUTION YOU SHOULD NEVER MAKE

Each year, millions of Americans make the resolution to go on a diet on January 1st. Many lose weight . . . and then gain it back. Listen up! We want you to make the resolution to *never* diet again, because diets will cause you to *gain* weight. In fact, a study published in the *Journal of Consulting and Clinical Psychology* showed that teens who diet "are significantly more likely to gain weight and become obese" than teens who do not diet.[1] A Harvard study of 15,000 teens confirmed that teens who diet gain more weight than their non-dieting friends.[2]

Researchers say diets cause long term weight gain because diets:

▼ disrupt your body's normal appetite system

▼ create erratic eating patterns

▼ affect your metabolism

▼ set up a cycle of bingeing/restricting

23

Diets fail for two reasons. First, they don't cure the true, underlying causes of overeating, and second, they create unhealthy patterns. The reality is that eating less and exercising more, though it seems like the slower road to weight loss, is truly the *only* road. Proverbs 14:12 tells us, "Before every man there lies a wide and pleasant road that seems right but ends in death" (TLB). That wide and pleasant road would be "dieting" when it comes to the subject of losing weight! So though diets may seem like a good way to deal with a weight problem, they are more likely to hurt your body and leave you bigger than ever. Alternatively, our goal follows the Lose It For Life plan—to help you restore a healthy relationship with food and bring you back to what God originally intended for your body's health.

Sometimes we think food is the problem. But really, food was created by God for pleasure and health, and it was created "good"! Eating should be a joyful, pleasant experience. You should be able to pause and actually taste each bite, enjoy the conversation of friends while you do so, and leave the table satisfied. Diets, on the other hand, introduce a lot of stress to the food relationship and eating in general. You have to always count calories, or carbs, or settle for one food while wishing for another. It makes eating a much less pleasurable experience.

This isn't something new or surprising to God—He created us and He created food. If anyone knows what that relationship *should* look like, it's our Creator! In fact, when God wanted to warn His people once in the Old Testament about a terrible future awaiting them if they continued to disobey His laws, He described the impending disaster and the feelings people would have in these terms: "They will eat their food in anxiety and drink their water in despair" (Ezekiel 12:19).

That sounds like a diet to me! The diets I've been on made me hungrier than ever and wishing for the days when I could just eat what I wanted,

## SOMETIMES WE THINK FOOD IS THE PROBLEM.

when I wanted. It felt like I was being punished, and I resented my friends who ate as they pleased. I felt anxiety that the food I was eating wasn't even enough to get me through until bedtime without starving, and that despite all the effort and hunger and telling myself no, the whole experience would likely amount to only a very slow weight loss.

Ever notice that the word "diet" starts with the word "die"? As in, this diet is killing me?

Yet even in the middle of the curse of my dieting, God was beginning to teach me, just as I hope He's teaching you now—to seek real freedom! And as an aside to stressing about why the weight isn't coming off faster when you are eating a salad instead of a cheeseburger, take this perspective to heart: You didn't become overweight because of just one "bad" meal, and you won't lose all your weight after eating one "good" meal either. Lose It For Life is a blessing, not a curse. And the blessing of Lose It For Life is that it frees you forever from diets. You won't eat your food in anxiety, or feel despair that the program is too difficult to live by forever. Eating the best, healthiest foods, and using moderation with the less-than-healthy ones, will help you have more energy while remaining at a healthy weight. Say goodbye to dieting, because this program is about making the right food choices, not depriving yourself. We wouldn't do that to you! Whether you're at a pizza party or at home studying, you're going to know how to make wise choices. No more "die"ting, because this weight loss program is about *living!*

## YOU NEED TO READ

*"Be careful about reading health books. You may die of a misprint."*

Mark Twain's tongue-in-cheek warning reminds us of an important fact: If you take the time to read information that pertains to your health, you'll be more motivated to apply what you've read. So, it's time to start reading labels. A lot of foods out there *seem* healthy and even promise to be lowfat, or sugar-free, or low-carb, but . . . THAT DOESN'T MEAN THEY ARE GOOD FOR YOU. Reading labels will help you understand how to choose the right foods and also spot the wrong ones. On the following page is a sample label to better understand the nutritional information provided[3]:

## FAST FOOD LABEL FACTS

*Serving sizes (1).* This amount is defined as the portion of food that is "customarily" consumed. This amount may be very different than what you *actually* eat and consider to be a

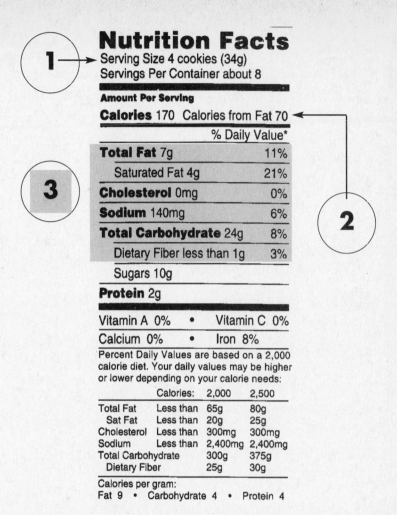

**Nutrition Facts**

Serving Size 4 cookies (34g)
Servings Per Container about 8

**Amount Per Serving**

**Calories** 170  Calories from Fat 70

| | % Daily Value* |
|---|---|
| **Total Fat** 7g | 11% |
| Saturated Fat 4g | 21% |
| **Cholesterol** 0mg | 0% |
| **Sodium** 140mg | 6% |
| **Total Carbohydrate** 24g | 8% |
| Dietary Fiber less than 1g | 3% |
| Sugars 10g | |
| **Protein** 2g | |

| | | | |
|---|---|---|---|
| Vitamin A  0% | • | Vitamin C  0% | |
| Calcium  0% | • | Iron  8% | |

Percent Daily Values are based on a 2,000 calorie diet. Your daily values may be higher or lower depending on your calorie needs:

| | Calories: | 2,000 | 2,500 |
|---|---|---|---|
| Total Fat | Less than | 65g | 80g |
| Sat Fat | Less than | 20g | 25g |
| Cholesterol | Less than | 300mg | 300mg |
| Sodium | Less than | 2,400mg | 2,400mg |
| Total Carbohydrate | | 300g | 375g |
| Dietary Fiber | | 25g | 30g |

Calories per gram:
Fat 9  •  Carbohydrate 4  •  Protein 4

single portion. For example, a serving size on the label might say "5 chips," but how many do you actually eat? It's also wise to compare the serving size on the label with the serving sizes listed on this meal plan, which is based on the government's food guide pyramid. For example, you may think one bagel is equal to a single serving of grains. Yet the label on a bagel from the grocery store may state that *half* of one bagel is one serving. So if you ate the whole thing, you

## Say What?

The FDA (Federal Food and Drug Administration) regulates the food industry and requires accurate and truthful ingredient labels be used on all consumable products. They also make sure any claims made on the package are backed up by scientific proof, such as, "This food promotes a healthy heart."

The FDA *does not* regulate the over-the-counter diet pill or food supplement industry. These supplements, powders, and pills *do not* have to be scientifically proven, *do not* have to contain the ingredients listed on the label, and *do not* have to be proven safe!

would need to count the entire bagel as two servings. (And watch out in restaurants and coffee shops, because a larger bagel or muffin may actually be somewhere between 4–6 servings.)

*Calories/Calories from Fat (2).* Eating too many calories causes weight gain and obesity, but foods high in fat are also high in calories, which will make you feel sluggish and tired. Look for foods that do not get the majority of their calories from fat.

*Nutrients (3).* The top portion of every food label consists of the nutrients you want to limit in your diet: fat, cholesterol, and sodium. If any single food has 20 percent or more of the daily value of these nutrients, it's not a healthy choice. The middle portion of the label speaks to the carbohydrates, sugar, fiber, and protein within the food. The healthiest choices are foods low in sugar and high in fiber.

Other nutrients to look for include calcium, iron, and other vitamins and minerals that pro-vide real health benefits, including warding off disease. Pay special attention to your calcium intake, because calcium turns on the fat burning mechanism in your

## CALCIUM TURNS ON THE FAT BURNING MECHANISM.

metabolism and strengthens your bones at the same time, which is critical in your teen years.

## HOW MUCH IS ENOUGH?

One key to weight loss is knowing exactly how many daily servings of each food group you should be eating. The U.S. government recommends female teens consume 2,200 calories each day. Some of you might think this is an awful lot of calories to eat, but keep reading!

### RECOMMENDED DAILY SERVINGS
### FROM THE FOOD GUIDE PYRAMID

| Grains | Vegetables | Fruits | Milk | Protein |
|--------|------------|--------|------|---------|
| 9 | 4 | 3 | 3 | 2.4 |

Besides reading labels and checking the portion size listed, you will need to compare those figures to the serving size we recommend here and make any adjustments you need to.

| GRAINS | FRUIT |
|---|---|
| ½ cup pasta or rice | 1 medium piece of fruit |
| ½ cup cooked cereal | ½ cup chopped fruit |
| ½–¾ cup ready-to-eat cereal | 4 ounces (½ cup) juice |

| VEGETABLES | MILK |
|---|---|
| 1 cup raw | 1 cup milk or yogurt |
| ½ cup cooked | 1 ounce cheese |
| | ½ cup cottage cheese |

| PROTEIN |
|---|
| 3 ounces meat, poultry, or fish |
| 2 ounces tofu |
| 2 tablespoons peanut butter |

When you have some time, spend a little while in the kitchen measuring your food to get an idea of what these serving sizes look like. If you know what half a cup of cooked rice looks like on a plate, or where eight ounces of milk comes to in a glass, you'll be more careful with your portion sizes.

Eating 2,200 calories on this meal plan is recommended for teens who are maintaining a healthy weight and are active. This plan has enough calories to stay healthy without starving. To get the most out of this plan, concentrate on trading out high-fat, high-sugar foods for healthier options. Less than five milligrams (mg) of fat or sugar per serving means the food choice is pretty healthy.

3 ounces of meat, poultry, fish, or tofu = 1 deck of cards

Fruits, 1 medium piece (1 serving) = a tennis ball

Medium sweet potato = a computer mouse

1/2 cup pasta = half a tennis ball

1 ounce of cheese = 4 dice

1 teaspoon of fats (peanut butter, butter, or margarine) = the tip of your thumb

## THE ALL-THESE-IN-3's MEAL PLAN

If you are significantly overweight and not active at all, you will probably want to cut back on the number of servings of grains listed here, but don't go below three servings a day or you'll deprive your body of nutrients it needs!

## RECOMMENDED DAILY SERVINGS
## FROM THE FOOD GUIDE PYRAMID

| Grains | Vegetables | Fruits | Milk | Protein | Fat |
|--------|------------|--------|------|---------|-----|
| 9 | 4 | 3 | 3 | 2.4 | 3 |

*OK, if you twist my arm, you can have more than three servings of vegetables in a day.

Having three servings of each food group will get you into a healthy range to maintain your metabolism, fight cravings, and start burning fat. Focusing on increasing the servings of fruits and vegetables is a great trick for weight loss, because every time you eat something healthy, there's less room in your stomach for something that's not. On our plan, you don't have to swear off chocolate or ice cream forever—you just have to focus on eating a healthy variety of foods that includes plenty of produce.

Adults may encourage you to eat more because "you're a growing girl!" But did you know that people ages 9–18 only need an additional 25 calories per day to support growth?[5] (For the average teen who is somewhat active, this means a total of about 2,225 calories a day is sufficient).

I am currently in a maintenance phase. To keep myself accountable, I keep a dry-erase board on my fridge with a "scorecard" that looks like this:

D ————

F ————

V ————

D stands for dairy, F for fruits, and V for veggies. My biggest challenge right now in maintaining a healthy weight involves remembering to eat enough fruits, vegetables, and dairy every day. It's so easy to assume I'm eating healthily, only to realize later I've been off track. But I know that if I'm eating six servings of fresh produce a day, I don't have near as much stomach-room for other foods, so my intake of grains and proteins is automatically placed within moderate amounts. If I was trying to lose more weight, however, I'd track those food groups too.

I also like using these codes since no one knows at first glance what they are. Every time I have a serving of that particular food group, I mark off a box. You can use the same system by carrying around a small notepad in your purse or pocket, tracking in your planner, or anywhere else.

Keeping track of your servings like this is a simple but potent motivator. I experience these benefits every day:

▼ I have to be honest about what I am eating. I can't hide from the fact that if I didn't get my six servings of produce in, I filled that stomach-space with other foods that were probably not as healthy.

▼ I know right away when I'm off track—I don't wait for the scale to register a gain.

▼ It eliminates "indecision eating." I'm less likely to open the pantry and stare blankly, wondering what I "should" eat. I already *know* I need to eat my servings of fruits and veggies.

▼ I don't feel deprived. I'm not carrying a list around of foods I *can't* eat. I'm carrying around a list of foods I've *got* to eat. It's a subtle difference that makes a big impact psychologically.

## Eat In 3's Too

Another great trick from the All-These-in-3's meal plan is to combine three food groups into every meal or snack. For example, if you eat an apple, add a tablespoon of peanut butter onto it, and wash it down with a glass of milk. That gives you fruit, a little protein, a healthy fat, and dairy. Eating this way keeps blood sugar more stable. You'll stay full longer and probably eat less later. So you may feel weird having three food groups at every snack or meal, but the payoff is that, overall, you'll eat less calories by eliminating blood sugar crashes and pick-me-up snacks. And remember, you want to focus on adding healthy foods into your meal plan and not saying no to yourself all the time.

> ### Protein Snacks
> Snacking on protein may help you feel full up to forty minutes longer than snacking on carbs alone.[6]

## The Diet that Can Make You Flunk a Test

Low-carb diets are nothing new. In the 1860's a low-carb book was published and titled, *Letter on Corpulence*. We're guessing the publisher didn't win any awards for coming up with that title!

Everyone's going on low-carb diets and losing weight . . . so why shouldn't teens do it too? First, low-carb diets frequently push you to give up dairy, which is a bum deal for teens. And because carbs are a source of glucose, the fuel for your brain, low-carb diets can make it hard for you to study

One of the most common mistakes teens make is cutting out dairy in order to lose weight. Recent studies have shown that consuming three servings of dairy every day significantly boosts your body's ability to burn fat. The calcium in dairy foods works better than calcium supplements. It allows your body to turn on the chemicals that burn fat and turn off the ones that store fat. In a study from the Nutrition Institute at the University of Tennessee, dieters who took in 1200–1600 milligrams of daily calcium lost 70 percent more weight than those who concentrated on only cutting calories.[7] So, never eliminate dairy foods from your diet to lose weight. Instead, concentrate on finding low-fat and low-sugar choices.

The FDA *does not* regulate the over-the-counter diet pill or food supplement industry. These supplements, powders, and pills *do not* have to be scientifically proven, *do not* have to contain the ingredients listed on the label, and *do not* have to be proven safe!

Another reason dairy is so critical right now is that your body is storing calcium in your bones like crazy. By the time you reach your thirties, that function is done—your bones have basically stored all the calcium they can from your diet. So you will either be at risk for osteoporosis or have a strong, healthy body. Think about it: When you're a little old lady, you won't want to spend your days at the retirement home watching TV and eating green gelatin while you nurse a broken hip along! So have another glass of milk!

and perform well on tests. Second, low-carb diets can make you feel more sluggish and less interested in a brisk walk or good workout. Finally, the long-term effects of a high-protein, low-carb diet are unknown.

There is an upside to this low-carb trend, however. More variety is being offered in restaurants and fast food places, and the new menu choices rely less on refined carbs and more on fruits and vegetables. Low- carb choices that consist primarily of natural, unprocessed produce are a great way to boost weight loss, satisfy your appetite, and power up your immune system.

So the million dollar carb question of "To carb or not to carb?" has a pretty rich answer! Eat carbs, but make sure they are the whole-grain, fiber-packed choices, and eat them as a part of a balanced program, such as the All-These-in-3's program. To find out if a product is made with whole grain, when you read the label, look for the words "whole wheat" or "whole grain" to be first on the list of ingredients, or at least within the first few ingredients. Some breads claim to be "wheat bread," but that doesn't mean they are made with *whole* wheat. Pretty sneaky, huh? Be vigiliant, because the carbs in refined products that have white flour and white sugar will raise insulin levels that protect your stored fat.[8] Also, because many products for carb counters are high in fat, they contain even more calories than the foods they replace![9]

## YOUR BODY'S BUILT-IN CALORIE COUNTER

Hands up if you've noticed we haven't told you to start counting calories. That's right! Because counting calories is a real pain. Most of us have trouble remembering our schedule every day, let alone the calories from every gram of food we've eaten. The truth is, we don't have to count calories, so we won't. (That being said, recording your food intake and then calculating your total calories eaten, even for a few days, can be a real eye-opening experience.) Good thing for us that our bodies come with a preprogrammed, state-of-the-art calorie counter. It's a highly sensitive instrument that sends quiet signals when you've eaten just enough, not enough, or a bit too much. And what is this amazing tool, exactly?

Hunger! Most of us who have weight problems have become desensitized to the delicate signal of hunger. We eat when we're not hungry (finishing off everything on our plate so we won't waste the food), then join friends at a coffee shop for a creamy, sweet frappucino. (Consider it a candy bar in a cup.) The only time it's OK to let ourselves get hungry is on Thanksgiving when we grouch around all morning waiting on the turkey to get done, then yell at everyone to pass the potatoes so we can go lie on the couch. (And don't even try the carbo-loading excuse for the shopping marathon the next morning. Been there, bought that.)

> *Hungry?*
> **Your body is less likely to store food as fat if you eat only when you are physically hungry.**[10]

Our culture believes hunger is the enemy of weight loss. Hunger is considered a terrible thing that must be avoided . . . because hungry people eat, so if you're never hungry, you won't eat . . . right? WRONG. Sorry to break it to you, but this is part of the reason we have weight problems. As I researched this book, I have collected dozens of weird and wacky tips from teens about avoiding hunger—everything from chewing sugarless gum to punching yourself in the stomach. (Please do not try this at home, people . . . those teens surely swung too high and hit their head first.) Every diet supplement sold on the market out there promises you can lose weight "with no hunger!" But the truth is, *hunger can be your best friend when you're losing weight!*

Hunger is the God-given signal to feed your body, and when you carefully listen for your appetite's signals, you won't overeat. One of the main reasons experts think diets make people gain weight is that diets disrupt the normal appetite cycle. *Your body is designed to function at its best if you eat only when you're hungry, and stop as soon as you feel satisfied.* If you begin listening to your body's cues on hunger, today, you might even begin to see a difference by next week! Hunger is one of the best guides in keeping your food intake reasonable and well-matched to your energy expenditures.

And if you think "just one bite" doesn't really matter when you eat past "full," consider these facts:

▼ When you eat past full and your body stores the extra calories as fat, your fat cells will swell up to six times their minimum size and begin to multiply. Researchers don't think fat cells *ever* go away, even if you lose weight! (They shrink in size, but not in number.)[11]

▼ It takes a million fat cells to store the calories in just one Life Saver.[12]

So that one extra bite when you know you're full can add a few million fat cells! Aagh!

Hunger pains can keep you on the right track of eating just enough for your body to function at its best while letting go of excess weight. But have you ever had the feeling *I've just got to eat!* even though you *knew* you weren't really hungry? So what's that all about? One word: *punk'd*. My friends, this is what happens when your appetite gets punk'd by your own blood sugar.

## What Real Hunger Is (and Isn't)[13]

| Real Physical Hunger | False Hunger |
|---|---|
| Builds gradually | Hits suddenly; "starving" |
| Stomach starts to rumble and growl | There is no real physical feeling |
| Feel full and you stop eating | Overeat even if you feel full |
| Different foods will satisfy | Crave very specific food; nothing else satisfies |
| Need to eat but can wait | Want to eat now to ease whatever is happening |
| Eat and feel fine | Eat and feel guilt and shame |
| 4–5 hours since last meal; need energy | Upset and want to eat now |
| Choose foods purposefully | Automatic or absentminded eating |

> **STOP SOONER. SINCE IT TAKES YOUR BRAIN AT LEAST TWENTY MINUTES TO GET THE "FULL" SIGNAL FROM YOUR STOMACH, PRACTICE STOPPING BEFORE YOU ARE COMPLETELY FULL. YOU CAN SAVE AT LEAST 100–200 CALORIES EVERY DAY DOING THIS—WHICH CAN ADD UP TO AN INCREDIBLE 20 POUNDS A YEAR![14]**

We've learned that hunger isn't the enemy—blood sugar swings are. When your blood sugar swings from high to low, you "crash" and want to eat even though you're not really hungry yet. Ever seen or read about a meth lab in the news? Meth labs are usually secret places where people convert ordinary chemicals into a highly potent drug. Well, your body has its own type of meth lab, although the drug that it produces is blood sugar. Blood sugar is probably the most in-demand substance on the planet, along with oxygen and water. Blood sugar can make you feel energized or withdrawn, sluggish or hyper. And every day, you supply your personal lab with the ingredients necessary to create this potent substance.

Imagine this lab is operated by a group of scientists. They demand more ingredients every 3-4 hours. Their job is to make energy called blood sugar to keep you feeling good and help you stay alert for study hall. So you send them ingredients—say a lean lunch of grilled chicken over stir-fried veggies—and they get to work. But it's hard work turning a complex meal like this into energy, and it takes them some time to do it. Meanwhile, they send out a messenger called insulin to deliver the much-needed energy to the cells. The scientists work hard and produce a steady amount of energy for several hours. But then they run out of raw materials and demand more.

This time you eat a snack of cookies and a soda. Woo-hoo! It's an instant blood sugar high! It's so easy to convert these foods into quick energy. Those scientists dump out all the energy at once and cause a massive spike in your blood sugar level. And those scientists then stop working until the buzz wears off. Next, they send out their errand boy, insulin, to store the excess sugar (because there was way more than you really needed) as fat. These scientists love storing fat! It can become habit-forming to spike your blood sugar, the crash, and

> *Spice it Up!*
> Add a quarter teaspoon of cinnamon to your breakfast cereal or fresh fruit smoothie. This spice may help improve your body's response to insulin and give you more stable blood sugar.[15]

then do the whole process again. It's a tough habit to break, because waiting for true hunger in the midst of a blood sugar crash can be very hard. But if you can get into the habit of controlling your blood sugar and wait for true hunger, you will shed weight for good.

## Foods That Punk Your Body

When reading labels, look for foods that have less than five milligrams of sugar per serving. These foods are less likely to cause blood sugar spikes and are also referred to as "low glycemic" foods. Those foods with a low glycemic index (GI) are beneficial because they satisfy hunger pains and reduce cravings, besides allowing for a slower, steadier rise in blood sugar after eating. Furthermore, studies demonstrate improved weight loss and a better sensitivity to insulin when low glycemic foods are consumed. Lastly, your performance in sports and workouts will improve with these types of healthier, lower-sugar foods.

A low GI lifestyle would mean the following changes:

### Incorporating a low GI Lifestyle

| Increase | Decrease |
| --- | --- |
| Fresh fruits, vegetables | Refined carbs |
| Whole-grain bread | Sugar-sweetened products |
| Unsweetened whole-grain cereals | Desserts |
| Lean meats | All whites: flour, sugar, pasta, potatoes |
| High-fiber foods | Low-fiber foods |

It's especially easy to *drink* too much sugar. Eliminate all extra sugar by avoiding the most obvious ones, such as sweet tea, coffee drinks made with sugar, and sodas. It's been estimated that drinking soda can increase your weight by fifteen pounds in a year. So, cut the soda and you might lose about a pound a month! However, also watch out for sports drinks like Gatorade or Powerade and juices and fruit smoothies. Though these may seem like healthy alternatives, they, too, are full of sweeteners and may actually hurt your weight loss journey rather than helping.

Food manufacturers use many different products to sweeten processed foods, even ketchup! Again, remember, if you see that a food has more than five milligrams of sugar per serving, check the label for these hidden sweeteners:

▼ Fructose

▼ High-fructose corn syrup

▼ Sucrose

▼ Glucose

▼ Maltodextrin

▼ Maltose

Seeing these sweeteners on the label doesn't mean you can't eat that food. But you should *limit* the amount you eat. Focus instead on getting some high-quality, low GI sources of nutrition into your plan for the day. An interesting fact about artificial sweeteners is that scientists are still researching whether these replacements might actually *create* more cravings for sweets! A study in the July 2004 *International Journal of Obesity* reported that rats fed artificial

*Fiber Facts*

**Fiber is a potent weight loss weapon because it keeps you full longer, besides keeping your blood sugar steady. It also helps fight constipation naturally. Take our advice on this one: It's better to eat an extra apple than take a laxative and hope it doesn't kick in on the bus!**

sweeteners gained more weight than rats who didn't. Until there's a solid conclusion, we recommend you use moderation with artificial sweeteners, which includes diet sodas.

## THE FAT THAT'S *ALL* THAT

I can hear the objections already: "You actually want me to *eat* fat? Are you crazy? Don't you know I'm reading this to *lose* my fat?" Don't freak on me here, because the truth is, you've got to eat fat to burn it. It's crazy, but it's every bit as true as the old saying that you've got to kiss a lot of frogs before you find your prince. Except that this is going to be a lot easier. And you won't have to check caller ID before every call either.

Studies have shown that the amount of fat Americans are eating has *decreased* over the past few decades, while our rates of obesity are climbing.[16] Fat in our diet is not the sole enemy—in fact, *eating healthy fats can promote weight loss.* So it's important to know the difference between fats . . . as in what's healthy fat, and what's not?

There are two basic types of fat: saturated and unsaturated. When you read the food labels, you'll see the amount contained in each serving. Saturated fat gets its own line on the label because these fats are bad news. You want to limit your consumption of these whenever possible. However, the worst

# THE WORST FAT IS TRANS FAT.

fat is trans fat, which will not be required to be listed on the food label until January 1, 2006. However, many manufacturers are already starting to put that information on the food label. Trans fat results when the food manufacturer waves its magic wand over fat and turns it into some strange mutated fat with a very long shelf life. (Well, maybe it's a little more complicated than that, but you really don't want to sit through a lecture about the life cycle of corn oil, do you?) Trans fats are chemically modified so that food companies can make more money because their products stay fresh on the shelf for a longer period of time. However, big money for businesses can mean bad health for you. The ingenuity of scientists is great when it puts a man on the moon, but not when it puts cheese in a can. Basically, all you need to know is to avoid foods that have "hydrogenated or partially hydrogenated oil" listed as an ingredient.

Healthy fats are *un*saturated. These are found naturally in foods and have not been chemically altered. Fats in avocados, nuts, olive oil, flax seeds, and some types of fish are all healthy fats. Eating unsaturated fats can:

▼ give you healthy skin

▼ boost your body's immune response

▼ contribute to regulating your menstrual cycle

▼ improve your brain and nervous system

▼ help improve insulin response

Fish oil supplements are a great source of healthy fats, but if you decide to add them into your diet, buy the enteric-coated variety (meaning the supplement dissolves in your intestines and not your stomach), and take them before bed. Fish oil capsules are notorious for causing "fishy burps." Another way to gain the benefits of healthy fat is by incorporating ground flaxseed into your diet. You can do this by adding it to cereals and other recipes. I sprinkle about one teaspoon of ground flaxseeds into my food almost daily. I saw a report on TV once that stated children who had flax seeds with their breakfast performed much better on tests at school that day. I figure it can't hurt to try, right?

## WEIGHT LOSS IN A BOTTLE

Psst . . . over here! I've got a magic weight loss supplement! It's in a bottle, doesn't have any calories, and it will help you lose weight! Believe me? You should—I'm talking about water! We know you've heard it before: "Drink eight glasses of water a day." To be honest, no one is really sure where that recommendation came from, but it sounds good, so we say it. In reality, you want to drink water until you are satisfied, but not gorged. Everything you take into your body should be taken in moderation, even the good stuff.

Yet water may be the only real weight loss in a bottle program available. Granted, it's *not* true that water can flush fat from your system, anymore than ironing your thighs will get rid of cellulite (that doesn't work). Your body *needs* water to function and burn fat; water also provides energy to your muscles. Water is a great substitute for sugar-sweetened soda or sports drinks. And a very interesting finding in a recent study published in the *Journal of Clinical Endocrinology and Metabolism* showed that drinking water causes your metabolism to rise slightly.[18] Experts believe one reason is that the body must heat the water.

Many people complain about not being able to get enough water into their daily routine. I recommend you get your water in on schedule, then supplement at meals and during workouts. Here's one plan:

| | |
|---|---|
| Before breakfast | 12 ounces |
| Before lunch | 12 ounces |
| After school | 12 ounces |
| Before dinner | 12 ounces |
| Before bed | 4 ounces hot decaf tea* |

## SURVIVAL TACTICS

There are moments and hours and days you will falter as you change your eating habits. All we ask is that you don't give up! This program isn't a two-week effort or even a two-

---

\* This is my own personal agenda. You don't want to disturb your sleep with bathroom trips, but establishing a comforting bedtime ritual that doesn't include eating is a great technique to help you slim down with ease. Besides, many decaf herbal teas also offer powerful antioxidants to boost your health and well-being.

year deal—it's a lifestyle change. So take the challenges as they come and do your best to follow the program, but if you mess up, just pick yourself up and get right back into it! Study the scenarios below for some tried-and-true methods.

### There's Nothing but Junk to Eat

You're going to have situations every week where you're hungry, tired, and the only food available is real junk. That's OK. That's real life. If you forbid junk food entirely in these situations, you might set yourself up to binge later if you feel deprived. Here's how to deal:

▼ Always keep an emergency snack in your locker, purse, or backpack. Try for a low-sugar energy bar and piece of fruit or a small handful of nuts and a piece of fruit (and a bottle of water, of course). This trick *works* for me. I pass on junk food a lot these days because I know I've got a healthy snack ready whenever I need it.

▼ If you know you're going into a junk-food fest, eat a serving or two of fruits and vegetables before you go. Not only does this take the edge off your hunger, you'll have less room for the unhealthy choices. You'll be able to indulge a little without overloading.

▼ If you want to skip the food at the junk fest entirely, that's a great choice too, but just make sure you eat before you go . . . and that you don't build up resentment about not eating like "everyone else." Consider asking the hosts to provide healthier foods at the next get-together.

▼ Practice the principle of eating only when hungry and stopping when you're satisfied. When eaten in moderation, no food can make you fat. You won't have to worry that you've blown it if you use this guideline.

## Aunt Flow Comes to Visit

Many young women report overeating during the last week of their menstrual cycle, just before their period starts. Hormones, cramps, and mood swings can make it especially hard to eat right, especially if you like to use food for comfort! To get through this particular week without going to pieces, the experts recommend these four strategies:

1. *Get enough calcium.* Getting in 3–4 servings of dairy each day over several months will improve symptoms of PMS, including reducing food cravings, mood swings, and water retention.[19]

2. *Get plenty of exercise.* If you exercise regularly, you may experience less bloating, depression, and anxiety during your menstrual cycle.[20]

3. *Make time to socialize.* Get out of the house. If you're struggling emotionally, make an extra effort to connect with friends—at a coffee shop, the movies, or whatever. You want to avoid the temptation of being alone and miserable when there's a full refrigerator down the hall.

4. *Follow a healthy meal plan.* (And may I suggest the All-These-In-3's plan?) Eating right may reduce pain. Some doctors think the most common cause of abdominal-pelvic pain in adolescent girls may be irritable bowel syndrome and that poor diet is likely to blame.[21]

## You've GOT to Have Chocolate

If you crave a particular food, which often happens—especially during the menstrual cycle—you don't have to feel deprived or get depressed about it. It's OK to eat some of what's "forbidden" as long as you eat only when you are hungry, stop when you are satisfied, and try to include some healthy options with it. For example, if you're craving chocolate, read the labels to find the lowest-sugar choice (usually dark chocolate), and eat it along with a balanced meal of proteins and complex carbs such as vegetables. Remember, knowing that no food is forever off-limits will short-circuit the urge to binge.

So you know what to eat with your chocolate so that your blood sugar doesn't spike and crash, but do you actually know *how* to eat the chocolate? Most of us with weight problems need a refresher course. The proper technique for eating chocolate includes:

1. *Unwrap the candy, then smell.* Experts believe smell plays a powerful role in weight loss, and giving ourselves a moment to really enjoy the aroma of one *small* piece of chocolate will make it seem like a *larger* experience.

2. *Taste your chocolate, don't chew it.* Never chew chocolate! Chocolate should melt slowly.

3. *Close your eyes and breathe deeply.* Congratulate yourself. You've just enjoyed one small piece of chocolate more than most people enjoy an entire candy bar.

## FAMOUS LAST WORDS

(OK, not famous, but still!) You know how to read a label, what to look for, and when enough is enough. When these three principles are put into practice, you'll not only start to feel better, you'll see a difference in the way your clothes fit too! A healthy approach to eating brings so many benefits: fewer mood swings, improved mental performance, and more energy, to name a few. This is a big step, but we know you can do it! And please don't be afraid to seek help. In fact, please pray with me for guidance.

## A HEALTHY APPROACH TO EATING BRINGS SO MANY BENEFITS!

~

*Lord, letting go of unhealthy habits is like letting go on a flying trapeze—I need to know You're there to catch me! Sometimes I think I won't be able to do it, but I know I don't have to do it all today. I can make just one small step towards a new life. Help me to focus on those little steps rather than the big leaps. Help me to trust that what is waiting for me when I let go is better than what I was holding on to. You were intimately involved in creating me, and You are with me still. Thank You that I won't start this journey alone. Thank You for being the best lifestyle coach I could ever hope for.*

# three

# MOVE IT AND LOSE IT!

Getting More Activity into Every Day

And now for the workout portion of our program! Don't hit snooze on me just yet. I've got some great tricks up my sleeve for you in this section. I know some of you despise breaking a sweat. And I know some of you are way too comfortable on that couch to even think of getting up and hitting the gym. But I also know you'd like to be a smaller size by next summer. Are you with me? Let's get moving!

First, let's determine your daily activity level. Where do you fit in this chart?

### DAILY ACTIVITY LEVELS

| | |
|---|---|
| Sedentary | Little or no physical activity daily |
| Moderate | Less than 60 minutes daily |
| Active | 60 minutes activity every day |
| Vigorous | More than 60 minutes a day |

Although the average teen's calorie level has only increased by one percent in the past two decades, the number of overweight teens has nearly tripled.[1] Experts say the reason for the gain is more teens now fall into the "Sedentary" category. Our lives are built around comfort and physical ease. Even our pastimes involve very little activity, except for trips to the bathroom or refrigerator. Today's average teen spends 16.7 hours a week on the Net and 13.6 hours a week watching TV[2]—for a whopping total of thirty plus hours of leisure time. And those are hours where only their index finger get any exercise, be it punching the remote or clicking a mouse.

## YOUR GREAT-GREAT-GREAT-GRANDMA HAD IT GOING ON

In the old days, you'd have to walk to the creek for water and haul heavy buckets back to the house. Then you'd walk three or four miles to school and back to help your dad work the land till dinnertime. Dinner was usually fresh or canned vegetables from your garden, milk from your cow, whole wheat bread made from scratch, and maybe some poor chicken you wrung to death yourself.

Oh sure, everyone was thin and fit, but your parents also chose whom you married. (Maybe it wouldn't be such a bad trade-off to have to exercise if you at least got to choose your dates!) Interestingly, it used to be *good* to eat when stressed! Those people's bodies needed the extra fuel to compensate for the demands they faced, whether it was harvesting in a hurry before an early winter or walking through the snow or swimming a creek while holding shoes over their heads on the way to school.

But physical activity doesn't come naturally to many of us these days. If we want to see a lion, we turn on the nature channel. If we want water, we turn on the faucet. Our stresses are usually more mental, such as studying for entrance exams. Thus, eating more food doesn't help us anymore the way it used to help Great-Great-Great Grandma. We have to adjust our modern lifestyles and add exercise back in. Replacing sedentary activity (an oxymoron if I ever heard one!) with exercise is a dramatic step towards winning the battle against obesity forever.

**YOU CAN FEED YOUR MUSCLES THE BEST FOOD AND VITAMIN SUPPLEMENTS IN THE WORLD, BUT IF EXERCISE ISN'T PART OF THE PLAN, YOUR MUSCLES WON'T BURN UP THOSE CALORIES.[3]**

These days, experts recommend you get at least sixty minutes of physical activity every day. Activity can include exercise, but you aren't limited to workouts. *Any* type of physical activity you add into your day counts! Your goal is to be active for one hour a day, whether it's a thirty-minute workout *and* a thirty-minute walk through the mall, or a long soccer game on the lawn with friends, or even (gasp) housecleaning. The truth is, you don't have to develop Olympian-in-training exercise routines to improve your fitness, or lose weight. Exercise—even with just moderate exertion—produces a wealth of health benefits, according to a Medical College of Georgia researcher.[4] Any of the following could count toward your sixty minutes of physical activity today:

▼ walking the mall

▼ curling a dumbbell while on the phone

▼ running on the treadmill while watching TV

▼ dancing to music

▼ playing tag while babysitting

One clever trick that may help you reach the hour of power goal is to break up your exercising into smaller segments throughout the day. Perhaps you could add fifteen minutes on the treadmill to your morning routine, then fifteen minutes of light weight lifting when you get home from school. This tip brings weight loss for lots of people: Studies undertaken at the University of Pittsburgh revealed findings in 1995 that women who were told to exercise in ten-minute spurts four times a day exercised more and lost more weight than women told to exercise forty minutes once a day. Most of the women chose walking for their exercise. Those who exercised in short bouts throughout the day lost about 40 percent more weight than those who exercised in a single daily session.[5]

## THE VERY *PRIVATE* REASON WHY WORKOUTS FAIL

One of the most common reasons teens fail to stick to an exercise program is that they make exercise all about their weight instead of themselves. For instance, every time you get on the treadmill or dust off that kickboxing DVD, are you muttering under your breath, "This had better work. I am SO fat!"? And then, at every moment during the workout, are you criticizing the way your thighs bounce or your stomach jiggles? (I know of someone who worked out on a treadmill in front of a mirror . . . *naked*, so they could see every ounce of fat jiggle and "be motivated.")

When you take this path, workouts become all about your hatred of your body and your negative attitude about yourself. It's pretty depressing, and so you stop exercising. Honestly, if I had to work out naked, I'd probably hurl! (Not to mention being banned from my gym!) But I know that it's better to keep moving. So here's how to approach physical activity: Make exercise your *haven*, not your *punishment*. Play music that you love. Wear

> ### Never Quit!
> People often quit their exercise routines because they start their program working too hard for their current fitness level.[6]

clothes that feel really good. Use this time to talk to God, and let the stress and tension drip away. I have practiced this principle myself over and over, and it's helped me tremendously. I look forward to workouts more now, because I know I'll be able to let go of my hurts and disappointments and all the worldly pressure to "measure up."

To really make this principle work for you, you'll have to exercise mind control, which means you *stop* every negative thought. You either replace it with a positive mental note or just concentrate on something else. The Bible puts it this way: "We take captive every thought to make it obedient to Christ" (2 Corinthians 10:5).

Exercise isn't about trying to force yourself into someone else's size of jeans. Instead, view it as an environment that will allow you to reach your full potential. Instead of focusing on becoming "less" of something, you're becoming *more* of who God created you to be. It sounds like a subtle difference, but in reality it's huge! To coin Abraham Lincoln's phrase, "The doors of history swing on small hinges," those little thoughts you entertain can actually make or break your weight loss efforts.

## THE WONDER TWINS OF WEIGHT GAIN

# THE WONDER TWINS OF WEIGHT GAIN: DRINKING SODA AND WATCHING TV.

Ask any physician what the leading cause of teen weight gain is and you'll probably get the same answer I did. (When I interviewed a doctor for this book, he almost shouted this answer at me. Good thing there was a nurse nearby—this poor guy was so frustrated that he almost lost it!) But seriously, girls, there's a deadly duo in your very own home that is guaranteed to both pack pounds on your lovely frame and make fitness seem like an impossible goal. In

> *He who walks with wise men will be wise.*
> —PROVERBS 13:20 NASB

If you struggle with exercising, here's a fantastic tip: Find an exercise partner. I've seen people struggle with their weight for decades and then find success because they were held accountable and kept moving. It doesn't cost anything to have a friend who will exercise with you! But it will keep you from turning over and going back to sleep rather than getting up and moving.

If you don't have any friends or you live in a swamp or you're in a relationship that won't allow you to have friends, you should know that your excuses are nothing new! So when you are ready, overcome the excuses, get a partner, and realize that you just may have found the key to the long-term weight loss you have been looking for. So find a buddy to walk with. Don't be afraid to ask someone who works out regularly already. Walking with the wise makes you wise, but walking with anybody makes you fit!

fact, if you get nothing else out of this book other than to heed this warning, you'll have gotten much, much more than your money's worth.

So, what are these wonder twins of weight gain? (Dramatic pause.) *Drinking soda and watching TV.* Yep, that's it! A study in the *Archives of Pediatrics and Adolescent Medicine* showed a strong relationship between TV watching, soda drinking, and weight gain. The youths with the heaviest BMI were the ones who drank three sodas a day and watched three hours of TV a day. The conclusion of the study? More soda means more TV means bigger and bigger kids!

There are lots of unhealthy reasons this duo packs on the pounds: First, TV watching is a sedentary activity. Second, drinking sugar-sweetened sodas causes your insulin to spike, which promotes fat storage. Third, drinking sweet sodas doesn't fill you up the same way solid food does, so you'll probably be wolfing down snacks in addition to the soda. And when you're eating unhealthy snacks and consuming soda that makes you feel tired after the initial high, you are less likely to make a good choice about eating a healthy dinner or going outside for some exercise.

If you are nodding your head because you do this, understand, there's no patch we can sell you or special gum to cure the cravings you will feel if you try and break the habit (which we hope you will!). That being said, you don't have to go cold turkey. If you can do this, great; if not, begin by cutting back to no more than one a day of either soda or watching TV. That's already a huge step towards a thinner, happier you. And if that sounds too drastic, here's a step-down plan than can help right away. If you normally drink three sodas a day and also watch three hours of TV per day, try following a new schedule:

**Monday/Tuesday/Wednesday:**
Drink two sodas and watch two hours of TV per day
(or less if you can!).

**Thursday/Friday/Saturday/Sunday**
Drink one soda and only watch one hour per day.

**Following Monday and beyond:**
Switch to water and maintain a limit
of one hour of TV per day.

Don't forget you can make that hour of TV count towards your sixty minutes of daily physical activity by incorporating some smooth moves!

▼ Keep a basket of hand weights near the TV, and do some reps while you watch your show.

▼ During commercials, stand and stretch, do the stairs twice, and add in a few stomach crunches.

▼ Put a treadmill, stair climber, or any type of exercise equipment near the TV and get a workout in. Remember, even short bursts of ten minutes of activity at a time can really reshape your body.

## MUSCLE MATTERS

"But tell me the truth!" you say. "If I eat less, I'll still lose weight no matter what, right? So why exercise at all—it took me an hour to get my eyeliner on straight and you want me to go and ruin it?" Well, the truth is, yes, you will lose weight if you eat less, even if you don't exercise. But the important thing to note is that what you'll really be losing is *muscle!* That's right . . . most weight loss programs result in up to 50 percent of weight lost in the form of calorie-burning muscle tissue.[7] If you don't build exercise into your weight loss program, very likely each pound you lose will be half fat and half muscle.

This is really bad news for your metabolism, because muscle tissue burns fat. Every pound of muscle burns 30–40 calories a day. Muscle tissue is seven times more metabolically active than fat tissue![8] So let's say you lose six pounds on my uncle's Cheetos diet. Figure half of that weight was muscle. This means your metabolism would be shortchanged by about one hundred calories a day . . . which could add up to a potential regain of ten pounds in a single year! So, at the end of the year, you've lost six pounds and regained ten. And to add insult to injury, or cellulite to your thighs, when you regain the weight from the diet (and almost everyone will), the weight will be almost all fat. So not only will the scale read four pounds heavier than when you started, you're also ending up with *more* fat and *less* muscle, and your metabolism won't operate as well anymore without all that muscle.

*Exercise* is the key to preserving muscle, burning fat, and raising your metabolism. And keeping that weight off . . . permanently! Because exercise is critical for maintaining your svelte new body. Research shows that fewer than five percent of people who lose weight by dieting alone are able

> ## *Are You Average?*
>
> **Research shows that if you are the average teen, your parents were probably more fit at your age than you are right now.[9]**
>
> **(Ouch! We just *can't* let that happen, can we!)**

to maintain their lower weight for two years or more.[10] But those who exercise regularly are much less likely to have regained their weight.

So hopefully I've convinced you that cutting back on calories without exercising is a bad idea. How do you choose what to do? How do you know whether you should walk, run, or rollerblade? It's all up to you! Really, what exercise is best for you is as personal as picking out underwear. And truthfully, as long as you've got it on, I really don't care what you pick!

**IF YOU DON'T BUILD EXERCISE INTO YOUR WEIGHT LOSS PROGRAM, VERY LIKELY EACH POUND YOU LOSE WILL BE HALF FAT AND HALF MUSCLE.**

When it comes to exercise, there are as many opinions about the best exercise for losing weight as there are workout programs. But *what* you do isn't nearly as important right now as *just doing it*. If you're self-conscious about your size when it comes to going to the gym, try working out early in the morning. At that hour, usually only the most dedicated souls are working out—the type more likely to respect you for braving the gym. Or you can lock yourself in your bedroom with some fitness tapes. If you can't afford a membership at the gym or don't know where to start, ask a friend to go walking with you a few times per week. It's easier to feel more confident when you have a friend working out with you.

If you still aren't sure where to start with exercise, or if you want to find the right type of exercise, check out this handy quiz to determine your workout style.

## WHAT IS MY PERSONALITY?

### Part One: My Personality and Hobbies
(Circle the letter that most represents you.)

1. As a kid, the activities I liked best were:
   a. Gymnastics, cheerleading, jump rope, or dance classes
   b. Playing outside—such as building forts or lemonade stands, climbing trees, exploring the woods, etc.
   c. Competitive sports
   d. Playing with dolls, reading, coloring, or art projects
   e. Parties, playing with my friends

2. My favorite hobbies today are:
   a. Anything new and challenging
   b. Outside activities—gardening, walking the dog, watching the stars
   c. Tennis, card or board games, team and/or spectator sports
   d. Reading, movies, needle crafts, painting, or anything which provides an escape
   e. Group activities with friends—anything from a walking club or joining a book group to just talking

3. I get motivated to exercise if:
   a. I get a new exercise video or piece of equipment, or I try a totally new class
   b. I get a new piece of outside equipment, I discover a new walking or jogging path, or the weather is nice
   c. I'm presented with some competition
   d. I find an exercise that I get really into to the point that I forget my surroundings
   e. I exercise in a group

4. I prefer to exercise:
   a. Indoors
   b. Outdoors
   c. Wherever there's a competition
   d. Wherever I am not the center of attention
   e. In a gym or fitness center, not at home

## INTERPRETING YOUR SCORE (PART ONE)

If you circled mostly the letter "a" or there is not an emerging pattern within your choices, you are probably **The Learner.** You're always trying something new and welcome physical and mental challenges. You are most likely an "associative exerciser," meaning you focus on the way your body moves and feels when you exercise. Choose activities that help you explore new moves: aerobics classes, any form of dance, Pilates, seated aerobics, inline skating, skipping rope, fencing, or any other activity that attracts your interest.

If you circled mostly the letter "b," you would be classified as an *Outdoors Person*. Fresh air is your energizer. So why not include nature in your exercise routine? Try hiking, biking, nature walking, gardening, lap swimming, or cross-country skiing.

If you circled mostly the letter "c," you are classified as *The Competitor*. You naturally like one-on-one, competitive types of activities. Try fencing, cardio kickboxing, and spinning classes. If you excelled in or enjoyed a sport when you were younger, take it up again.

If you circled mostly the letter "d," you are classified as *Timid*. You're a "disassociate exerciser," meaning you fantasize or think of events in your life when you exercise rather than contemplating the exercise itself. You're more like a wallflower than a participant. You'll like mind/body activities like Pilates and stretching. Also try nature walking or hiking. You'll also probably love exercise classes. Sign up for classes such as aerobics, cardio kickboxing, seated aerobics, spinning, step aerobics, or water aerobics.

If you circled mostly the letter "e," you are classified as a *Social Butterfly*. As a people-person, you tend to prefer the gym to exercising in your living room. Try aerobics classes, kickboxing, seated aerobics, spinning classes, stretching, step aerobics, and water aerobics. For weight lifting, find a buddy or two and do circuit training.

## WHAT IS MY WORKOUT STYLE?
## WHAT ARE MY WORKOUT GOALS?

### Part Two: My Workout Style and Goals
(Circle the letter that most represents you.)

1. My primary exercise goal is:
   a. To lose weight or tone up
   b. To relax and relieve stress
   c. To have fun
   d. Depends on how I feel

LOSE IT *for* LIFE *for* TEENS

2. I prefer:
   a. A lot of structure in my workout
   b. Some structure, but not too much
   c. No structure
   d. Depends on my mood

3. I prefer to exercise:
   a. Alone
   b. With one other person
   c. In a group

## INTERPRETING YOUR SCORE (PART TWO)

If you circled mostly the letter "a" or a mixture of letters, you're classified as a **Gung-ho Exerciser**. You don't mess around when you work out. You're there to lose weight and tone up—period. You'll benefit most from doing a specific activity, like cycling, aerobics, or using an elliptical machine, treadmill, or stair climber, at a moderate intensity. For optimal weight loss benefits, you should burn 2,000 calories a week. One way to achieve this would be to perform thirty minutes of aerobic-based exercise daily, combined with three sessions of weight training per week.

If you circled mostly the letter "b," you would be classified as a Leisurely Exerciser. Your main exercise objectives are to relax and destress. To relax, try stretching. Studies have shown a direct relationship between physical activity and stress reduction. Hop on the treadmill or head outside and walk for five minutes, run slowly for thirty seconds, and then run fast for thirty seconds, repeating this sequence for about thirty minutes. Circuit weight training is another great interval workout. You do all your reps, then you rest, then you do a few more, and then you rest.

If you circled mostly the letter "c," you are classified as a *Fun-Loving Exerciser.* Fifty straight minutes on the treadmill is not your bag—there's no room in your fun-filled life. You'll be most likely to stick to activities that are already an integral part of your schedule. Grab your inline skates and circle the neighborhood. Put on your favorite music CD and dance around the living room. And you can make your weight routine more amusing by doing circuit weight training.

If you circled mostly the letter "d," you are classified as a Flexible Exerciser. Exercise turns you on, but routine doesn't. You'd rather fly by the seat of your gym shorts, which is fine. To add variety, use the elliptical machine one day, the treadmill the next, and the cross-country skiing machine the next.

## WHAT IS MY LIFESTYLE?

### Part Three: My Lifestyle and Schedule
(Circle the letter that most represents you.)

1. I have the most energy:
   a. In the morning
   b. In the middle of the day
   c. In the evening or at night
   d. My energy level fluctuates

2. I have the most time:
   a. In the morning
   b. In the middle of the day

    c.  In the evening
    d.  Depends on the day

3.  I'm most likely to:
    a.  Go to bed early and get up early
    b.  Go to bed and get up at the same time every
        day, but not particularly early or late
    c.  Go to bed late and get up late
    d.  Depends on the day

## INTERPRETING YOUR SCORE (PART THREE)

If you circled mostly the letter "a" or a mixture of letters, you're classified as a *Morning Dove*. You like to get chores out of the way as soon as you get up because that's when you have the most energy. Whether you go to the gym before you start your day or head outside for a dawn walk, you'll have an extra edge over those who hit the snooze button a few more times.

If you circled mostly the letter "b," you would be classified as a *Midday Duck.* You'd rather plop down on an exercise bike than in front of a sandwich when noon rolls around. Whether you're at home or work, exercise is a great way to break up your day.

If you circled mostly the letter "c," you are classified as a **Night Owl**. You haven't seen a sunrise since that all-night party in 1974. If you have more energy at night, use that time to exercise. Just don't do it too close to bedtime, or you'll have trouble sleeping.

If you circled mostly the letter "d," you are classified as a **Flexible Bird.** The best time of day for you to exercise

varies with your schedule. So just go with it and don't try
and set yourself up with an intense schedule. But do push
yourself to exercise as often as possible!

## WALKING YOUR WAY FIT

If you are sitting on the couch and worrying you aren't ready
for exercise, consider starting with this beginner exercise
program. Walking is one of the best exercises you can do to
get your body on track. You will need to commit to walking

### STRENGTH AND RESISTANCE TRAINING

If you decide to do strength training on the days
you aren't walking, check out these benefits! Figure
twenty minutes, two days a week. That's not a big
time investment for the dividends:

▼ strengthens and tones your muscles

▼ improves self-esteem and mood

▼ slows bone loss and increases bone density

▼ improves flexibility and mobility

▼ helps control blood pressure

▼ reduces the incidence of lower-back pain

▼ reduces joint and muscle injuries and
strengthens connective tissue around muscles

three times each week (we recommend Monday, Wednesday, and Friday). The only equipment you need is a good pair of walking shoes and a watch. A walking partner isn't necessary, but having one might make you more accountable!

For the first week, walk ten minutes each of the three days. Add an additional five minutes the second week to your walks. During the third week, add five minutes more. Continue this program of adding five additional minutes so that by week five you are walking thirty minutes, three times a week.

During week six, the routine gets bumped up to a new level. Add short sprints into the workout. Sprint (or walk as fast as you comfortably can) for up to one minute, then resume your normal pace for at least two minutes, then sprint again. Try and do this four times during your daily workout.

If you want to really see results, try one of the following:

▼ Add in light weight training on non-walking days for dramatic muscle sculpting.

▼ Work out early in the morning, before breakfast, at least once during the week.

▼ Introduce a new sport! Try jogging or rollerblading and following this routine for another six weeks.

## Burn, Baby, Burn!

To optimize the fat-burning potential of workouts, we recommend working up to exercising aerobically for at least thirty minutes at a time, 3–5 times per week. Many experts believe you must exercise between 20–30 minutes before your body will begin to burn fat effectively.

What *exactly* does "aerobic" mean? *Requires oxygen*—yep, that's what it means. A good rule of thumb is that if you can carry on a conversation but have a hard time carrying a tune, you are having an aerobic workout. In fact, voice coaches often use this technique to train rock stars for their world tours. The stars have to learn to sing *during* an aerobic workout so they can dance and sing on stage. It's a brutal training program, which might explain why lip synching is so popular! Even if you're not a rock star (yet), there are real benefits to aerobic conditioning:

▼ better ability to say no to extra food you don't need[11]

▼ reduce anxiety[12]

▼ help your brain release endorphins, the "feel good" hormones we all need

▼ improve learning[13] and memory[14] (if you remember to do it!)

▼ strengthen your immune system

▼ raise your metabolism

Even short bursts of activity throughout the day can increase your calorie burn up to a startling 500 calories or more per day. To make this technique work for you, try to get up once every hour for a 4–5 minute burst of activity—it works!

▼ Do standing squats as you blow-dry or curl your hair.

▼ Bring in the groceries for your mom.*

▼ Pace or march in place while you talk on the phone.

▼ Sweep, mop, or vacuum the floors.*

▼ Take the stairs instead of the elevator.

▼ Squeeze your buttock muscles and "zip in your abs" as you stand in line.

▼ Take the stairs . . . twice!

▼ Walk the dog.*

---

\*   Performing this activity may also increase your chances of borrowing the car this weekend!

# FAT-BURNING SECRETS OF THE PROS

Interval training, which professional athletes call *fartlek* (Don't laugh! That's the Swedish word for "speed play" and it's really what athletes call it. People, I could *not* make this stuff up!), is a potent fat-buster. A recent study compared the fat-burning effectiveness of a moderate intensity workout to a high intensity workout and found that using high intensity effort during your workout can cause a fat loss up to nine times greater than moderate exercise alone.[15] Workouts that make it easy to add short bursts of high intensity exercise include:

▼ walking

▼ running

▼ stair climbing

▼ cycling

▼ swimming

▼ aerobics

Before you incorporate high intensity intervals, you'll need to work first on getting into the habit of working out regularly. Speed intervals aren't for beginners who just got off the couch. Instead, save these intervals for challenging yourself after you've worked up to exercising several times a week for thirty minutes at a time. Also, high intensity bursts may not be good for you in a high-impact exercise. For example, if you're uncomfortable jogging or walking, save the high intensity work for a nonimpact activity such as cycling. Begin slowly and add one high intensity burst per workout. You can work up to several per workout as your fitness increases.

Here's what a high intensity workout would look like for someone who has been working out for a few months (for beginners ready for fartleking, just add *one* of these high-intensity bursts per workout):

| | |
|---|---|
| Warm-up: | 5 minutes |
| Walk at a moderate pace: | 4 minutes |
| Race-walk*: | 1 minute |
| Walk at a moderate pace: | 4 minutes |
| Race-walk: | 1 minute |
| Walk at a moderate pace: | 4 minutes |
| Race-walk: | 1 minute |
| Walk at a moderate pace: | 4 minutes |
| Race-walk: | 1 minute |
| Cooldown: | 5 minutes |

*Swing your arms faster and higher, take longer strides, and try to take faster steps.

Another way to incorporate high intensity training is to monitor your exertion and vary it throughout your workout. Some exercise machines will automatically do that for you, but it's pretty simple to do on your own as well. The Borg Scale for Rate of Perceived Exertion on the following page lets you assign a number to your effort. To use it, study your body and consider how hard you are working. Is your breathing heavy? Are you sweating? Do your muscles feel warm? Are they burning? Now rate how you feel.

## BORG SCALE FOR RATE OF PERCEIVED EXERTION (RPE)[16]

### Rating of Perceived Exertion Scale

| | |
|---|---|
| 0 | Nothing at all |
| 0.5 | Very, very weak |
| 1 | Very weak |
| 2 | Weak |
| 3 | Moderate |
| 4 | Somewhat Strong |
| 5 | Strong |
| 6 | |
| 7 | Very Strong |
| 8 | |
| 9 | |
| 10 | Very, very strong |

## HOW TO SPOT REDUCE

We've all seen those creams you're supposed to rub on that guarantee you'll lose inches off your thighs and rear. (So if they really work, how come your hands don't get smaller too?) In the real world, though, there's no such thing as spot reducing, unless you want to go under the knife. And even *that* is by no means perfect.

Popular spot reducing products also include ab rollers and thigh wizards. These usually do have modest effects, but when you exercise using a special bun burner machine or other spot reducing contraption, you should know that the fat burned during exercise, if any, will be taken from the

Sometimes working out can do more for you than just tone the body. Consider these two positives of improving fitness:

▼ Colleges are always looking for young women who show leadership potential as well as active involvement in their community. Think about signing up for a fundraising walk or half marathon. It's an awesome fitness goal that keeps you motivated for months, and it will look great on your college application!

▼ A study from California State University found that if you are prone to worry, especially in stressful situations such as exam week, working up a good sweat during a workout will help you feel better and experience fewer negative emotions than your friends who don't exercise.[17]

stores in your body overall. None of these contraptions can reduce the fat stored specifically in one area.

But special spot-specific exercises *can* help firm up various muscle groups, which in turn, will make that area look smaller. If you have a trouble spot (mine tends to run from my collarbone to my knees), investigate some quality pieces of equipment to add variety into your workouts. Resistance bands for thighs and rear and dumbbells for arms are probably the best investment, since they allow you to target a specific area, and are inexpensive. You can research other types of equipment, but beware of miracle promises. Any product that promises to take inches off your body without a lot of sweat and muscle-building exercise is likely a waste of money. When it comes to exercise products, less is more: The more realistic promises they make, the more realistic its benefits will be.

# Put It All Together

My personality type: _____
_____

My workout style is: _____
_____

My exercise goals include: _____
_____

My lifestyle/schedule type is: _____
_____

The best time for me to exercise is: _____

_____

_____
_____
_____
_____
_____
_____
_____
_____
_____

_____

_____

_____

_____

_____

_____

_____

_____

_____

_____

_____

_____

_____

_____

_____

_____

_____

_____

_____

~

*Lord, it's so hard to get motivated some days to
exercise, and yet when I do it, I feel great. I need Your help to care
for this body You've entrusted me with. You created me and know
my personality, my schedule, and my challenges. Would You
please make my workouts a blessing in my life, a time when I can
meet with You and be refreshed? Would You renew my spirit as
I renew my body through exercise? Thank You, Lord.
I love You. Amen.*

# four

# FEEL IT, DON'T EAT IT!

Identifying Emotional Eating Patterns and Finding New
Strategies for Coping—Without a Fork!

Wow—can you believe it? You're about halfway
through the book already! You've already learned
more about how to lose weight and keep it off than
most adults know. You've now been primed and positioned
for the three most critical steps in weight loss. This is where
the journey gets interesting, because these three steps have
*nothing* to do with food! I'm going to bring in some new tour
guides to walk us through this wilderness on our way to the
promised land. First, the founder of Lose It For Life, Stephen
Arterburn, shares his own weight loss story.

## A Flashpoint Moment
## that Changed Everything[1]

*I come from a family of fairly large people. At Thanksgiving dinner . . . almost everyone present was overweight, and everything on our table seemed to be either fried or served with gravy. I ate what was on my plate and never thought much about it, but looking back I can see that food, love, and relationships were definitely intertwined in my development. The result was that by the time I was twenty-two, I'd managed to pack 210 pounds onto my five-foot-ten-inch frame.*

*I was ashamed of my body, and it hurt to know that others were laughing at me. I felt I was destined to be heavy all my life, because, after all, I came from a heavy family.*

*But the summer before my senior year in college, when I had my picture taken for the yearbook, I experienced a flash-point that changed everything. When I received the picture proof, I was stunned to see the overweight, acne-pocked, oily-haired creature in the photograph. I was so ashamed of what I had become, until I realized I didn't have to stay that way. In that moment, I recognized the fact that I was responsible for how I looked, and I could make myself look different.*

*I had heard all the stories about people who lost weight only to regain it later. I was determined not to repeat that pattern because I knew that most people ended up heavier than they were when they started! Instead, I made gradual changes that caused me to see myself in a different light.*

*I began to walk every day. I learned to eat in different patterns. The flashpoint was instantaneous, but the resulting action took some time. With persistence, slowly but surely, the weight began to drop off, my waist narrowed, and the mirror stopped being my enemy.*

*First, I went down to 190 pounds and lived there for a while. A few years later I slimmed down to 175 and stayed at that weight for a few months. In my last stage of weight loss, I moved down to 160, the weight I maintain today.*

*The secret to weight loss, you see, isn't following rules or a plan—any of those will work temporarily. Permanent weight loss occurs when you change your heart and mind before you attempt to change your body.*

Steve just shared a secret to real weight loss that very few people will ever receive. Girls, understand this: The changes you make that will truly set you free from overeating are emotional and spiritual. Changing what you see on the *outside* means being willing to change what no one else but you can see on the *inside*. This reality is supported by medical literature. "Clinical studies show that you can diet and exercise all you want, but if your mind and emotions aren't engaged in the weight loss process, within two years you'll probably gain back any weight you lose."[2]

## THE TRUE TEST[3]

Most of us get into trouble with our weight when we get into trouble with our emotions. Fitness therapist Laure Redmond says, "People who suffer weight problems generally have emotional triggers that set unhealthy habits into motion."[4]

To find out if you are an emotional eater, take this twenty-question test. It's written by Dr. Linda Mintle, Steve Arterburn's co-author for the adult's guide to *Lose It For Life*. Dr. Mintle has been a counselor of weight related issues for twenty years and has helped thousands deal with the emotional side of weight loss. As Dr. Linda states in that book, "If you answer yes to any of these questions, chances are you are an emotional eater. This means that feelings often trigger your desire to eat. *When* you stop eating depends on *why* you are eating."

## FEELINGS OFTEN TRIGGER YOUR DESIRE TO EAT.

▼ Do I think about food often or all the time?

▼ Do I eat to relieve tension, worry, or upsets?

▼ Do I eat when I am bored?

▼ Do I continue to eat after I feel full, sometimes to the point of feeling sick?

▼ Does eating relieve my anxiety?

▼ Do I eat without thinking?

▼ Do I have to clean my plate?

▼ Do I eat in secret or hide food?

▼ Do I eat quickly, shoving in the food?

▼ Do I feel guilty after I eat?

▼ Do I eat small portions in front of people, but go back for more food when people aren't around?

▼ Do I binge (eat large amounts of food in a short period of time)?

▼ Can I eat one serving, or do I have to eat the entire amount (a bag of cookies, or the whole half gallon of ice cream)?

▼ Do I feel out of control and impulsive when eating?

▼ Do I eat when I am not physically hungry?

▼ Do I lie to myself about how much I really eat?

▼ Do I have trouble tolerating negative feelings?

▼ Do I have impulse problems in other areas of my life (shopping, gambling, sex, alcohol, pornography, drugs)?

▼ Have I been on numerous diets over the years?

▼ Do I experience constant weight fluctuations?

Ouch! Some of those questions really hit home. Has Dr. Linda been hiding out in your refrigerator too? The truth is, Dr. Linda is able to accurately pinpoint emotional eating behaviors *because they are so common.* Most studies of obese patients seeking treatment show that they eat in response to negative emotions and stressful events. The studies have also proven that emotional overeating has several distinct characteristics:[5]

▼ of an episodic nature (meaning this type of overeating is not the same as constant grazing; it is initiated by an event)

▼ often done in secret

▼ has nothing to do with hunger cues

▼ induced by different triggers for different people

▼ results in temporary relief from the negative trigger

▼ involves a high-calorie or high-carbohydrate food (Which explains why you never see anyone locking themselves in their room to binge on romaine lettuce!)

## Your Emotional Eating Patterns

To break free from emotional eating, you must monitor your emotional responses and eating patterns. Keeping a diary of your food will help you track overall food intake, which we talked about in Chapter Two, and also helps you to identify your own unique emotional eating patterns. Different triggers for overeating affect each person differently, and my reason for overeating may not be the same as yours. Keeping a diary will be crucial to pinpointing what is driving you to eat when you aren't hungry.

The facing page gives an example of how your food diary might look:

Can you begin to identify the emotional triggers this person struggles with? I would guess perfectionism (she needed to unwind after a performance-based event, then got mad at herself for doing it), and loneliness (she wanted to be a part of the group even when it meant sacrificing her own goals).

## Tracking Triggers

"Many kids indulge in junk foods because they haven't learned how to handle anxiety or depression . . . others are spending too little time with their parents and are trying to nurture themselves with food."[6]

So let's find out what *your* particular patterns are. By recording your food and feelings in the Food Diary at the back of the book (see page 171), perhaps you, too, will see common triggers emerge which fuel your emotional overeating.

# Food Diary

| Name: | | | Day: | |
|---|---|---|---|---|
| When I ate | What I ate | How much? | Was I Hungry? | Feelings |
| Breakfast 7:00 A.M. | Granola & Yogurt | 1 cup each | Yes | Have big test and it's important to eat breakfast |
| 9:30 A.M. | Candy bar | 1 | No | Relieved that test is over, needed to unwind |
| Lunch 12:00 P.M. | Hamburger & Fries | 1 20 | Yes | Frustrated for eating the candy bar, hopeless about losing weight |
| 4:00 P.M. | Energy bar & Apple | 1 each | Yes | Strong, hopeful. I can do this! |
| Dinner 7:00 P.M. | Spaghetti & Steamed broccoli | 2 cups | Yes | Peaceful, happy |
| 9:00 P.M. | Ice cream | 2 cups | No | Sad. Everyone in the family was eating it and I wanted some too. Depressed. |

## Pride

I put this one at the top of the list just because it seems like the most unlikely candidate for causing overeating. You'd think someone dealing with puffed up pride in themselves wouldn't be hiding in their room eating two dozen Twinkies, right? I will confess that I put this one at the top of the list because God showed me it was what *I* struggled with. (For the record, I never locked myself in a room with two dozen Twinkies . . . maybe enough chocolate to put the Easter Bunny out of business though!)

One day when I was praying about my struggle to accept myself with the same grace I accepted my friends with, God sort of nudged me and informed me that I had a lot of pride in my heart to hold myself to a higher standard than everyone else. "You don't *need* to look like a supermodel because you're *not* a supermodel" was pretty much what I thought He was saying. (Ouch. Thanks for reminding me.) Accepting myself the way I was and the life God was willing to give me meant I had to have the same standard for everyone (me included). If it's OK for others to have imperfections (and it is) then it's also OK for me. And I can't just fake it in public and then work like crazy in private. I have to let go and live life as I am.

> Let's just go ahead and be what we were made to be, without enviously or pridefully comparing ourselves with each other, or trying to be something we aren't.
>
> —ROMANS 12:6 (MSG)

## Anger

Dr. Linda Mintle tells us anger is the most reported emotion tied to overeating. (Now *that* makes me mad!) Why is it so difficult to control anger without reaching for food? It turns out anger sets off a complex set of chemical reactions in our bodies. Our muscles tense up for a confrontation, our brain's neurons go on overload, and we need an outlet fast! The brain has a hard time knowing when to turn off the flood of reactions to anger; it takes a major diversion to get us back under control and cooling off. Watching TV, reading a book, and eating—anything that wrenches our focus onto something else—are all possibilities for creating that outlet.

So food can feel good because it distracts us, refocuses us, and helps us cool down for the moment. But swallowing anger is as helpful as swallowing a fish hook. What looked enticing going down has a terrible price. Good thing for us, God's Word gives a solid foundation for dealing with this difficult emotion.

## ANGER MANAGEMENT 101[7]

### *Do . . .*

*Be slow to become angry—James 1:19*

*Stop and think before you answer when angry*
*—Proverbs 15:1-2*

*Forgive those who anger you—Matthew 6:14*

*Get to the source of your anger—Psalm 4:3-5*

*Give your anger to God—1 Peter 5:7*

*Stay away from angry people—Proverbs 22:24*

*Gain control over a quick temper—Proverbs 14:17*

### *Don't . . .*

*Go to bed angry—Ephesians 4:26*

Give full vent to your anger—Proverbs 29:11

Get caught up in name-calling—Matthew 5:22

Take revenge—Romans 12:19

Harbor anger—Colossians 3:8

Take offense—Proverbs 12:16

### Rejection

The frustration of being rejected solely based on appearance is nothing new, yet each instance can feel like a fresh wound. And interestingly enough, losing weight won't necessarily lessen this pain! As one girl shares, "When I was fat, I would walk into a restaurant and everyone would stare at me. I knew they were rejecting me because of my size. I hated it. Now I've lost weight, and when I walk into a room of people, I see them smile and act polite and it bugs me. I know they are still judging me by my size, not by who I am."

Rejection, be it in the form of a friend who abandons you on Friday night for a party you weren't invited to, or a classmate who makes fun of you, *hurts*.

▼ It *hurts* when people "moo" when you walk down the hall.

▼ It *hurts* when people sing the Jenny Craig song when they see you.

▼ It *hurts* when your brother calls you fat.

▼ It *hurts* when people laugh at you as you're eating.

When the pain becomes unbearable, it's so tempting to eat to soothe our nerves. The only problem is, your spirit never gets the food! It all goes straight to your hips and stomach. You're left with a hangover of guilt and shame, and less able to take the pain of rejection when it hits again. And it will. I know you're expecting a pep talk here, but the truth is, rejection is part of the everyday experience of humanity. And it is worse for some of us than others. But I've noticed a curious phenomenon about that, and I want to share it with you here: *Rejection is one of the most powerful tools God has to shape you for greatness.*

For one week, I want you to pay careful attention to every biography you read or see, and every major character in the Bible you can remember. Did you notice the people who are rejected more often have a destiny greater than their peers? It's unclear if the person rises to greatness because of the strength developed in overcoming adversity, or if the rejection just moves them down the path they wouldn't have chosen otherwise. No matter how it works, though, it *does* work. I can't make the teasing stop, and I can't reach through these pages and show you the path God is outlining for you. But I can pray for you and encourage you that all the pain of rejection you're experiencing doesn't mean you *are* a reject. It might just mean God has something incredible planned for you!

Here's what you can do:

▼ Develop and nurture your unique "outsider" perspective.

▼ Reach out to other outsiders—they may help you define your dreams.

▼ Stop coveting popularity: It might just cost you your destiny.

▼ Practice gratitude for the gifts that rejection brings: courage, vision, ambition, perseverance.

*Don't become so well-adjusted to your culture that you fit into it without even thinking. Instead, fix your attention on God. You'll be changed from the inside out. Readily recognize what he wants from you, and quickly respond to it. Unlike the culture around you, always dragging you down to its level of immaturity, God brings the best out of you, develops well-formed maturity in you.*

—Romans 12:2 (msg)

*But the Lord said to Samuel, "Do not consider his appearance or his height, for I have rejected him. The Lord does not look at the things man looks at. Man looks at the outward appearance, but the Lord looks at the heart."*

—1 Samuel 16:7

## Anxiety

A few years ago (and I'm not telling you how many), I was an actress. My agent called to tell me about an audition for a music video with a hot rock band. And, as you know, chicks in hot rock videos have to look really skinny, right? I didn't own a tummy-firming girdle or bun-lifting pair of underwear, and I decided I *had* to look smaller and firmer in my black leather skirt. So I did the only thing a reasonable teenage actress would do when given the chance to be in a hot rock video: I borrowed my dad's duct tape and wrapped my hips so tightly that I could only take three-inch steps (but I looked great!).

My plan was working fine until I heard the director wanted to shoot a poolside scene, so could everyone be ready to change into bikinis, please? Suffice it to say, there's only one way to get duct tape off, and it's not pleasant. *That,* my friends, is anxiety. I'm no stranger to this nagging, frightened little weasely emotion that is always pestering and prodding us to believe the worst is yet to come. If anger is the most reported emotion linked to overeating, anxiety is a close second. I love what Dr. Jill Hubbard, a counselor with the Lose It For Life Institute, says to us about anxiety:

> **TO DEAL EFFECTIVELY WITH OUR FEARS AND ANXIETY, WE NEED TO FACE THE TRUTH ABOUT OURSELVES AND GROW INTO A PLACE WHERE WE CAN ACCEPT WHO WE ARE.**

> To deal effectively with our fears and anxiety, we need to face the truth about ourselves and grow into a place where we can accept who we are. A lot of people dealing with anxiety have this ideal image that they are supposed to be more than they are. They think that if only they could get certain things under control, then they would be this great person. What's important to realize is that we don't need a ton of GREAT people running around in the world—we need people who are TRUTHFUL about themselves, more accepting. Then we are more able to entrust ourselves and our limitations to God and receive the promise of His being a refuge and safety in the midst of our fears and anxieties.[8]

*Cast all your anxiety on him because he cares for you.*

—1 PETER 5:7

## Jealousy

People eat out of jealousy when they compare themselves to others and only consider appearances. To assume being thin means happiness is to be deceived. Jesus tells us to "Stop judging by mere *appearances,* and make a right judgment" (John 7:24, emphasis added.) And Paul in Galatians 2:6 follows Christ by saying, "As for those who seemed to be important—whatever they were makes no difference to me; God does not judge by external appearance—those men added nothing to my message."

Jealousy is a very unproductive emotion; it leads to frustration and getting off God's path because you think you can "fix" the problem quickly. But if you can take your thoughts captive and refuse to compare yourself to others, you'll begin to unload the baggage that drives overeating. "For where you have envy and selfish ambition, there you find disorder and every evil practice" (James 3:16).

## Loneliness

"When I was full and had eaten as much as I could possibly eat, I felt like some part of me was full," said Angie. "Something that wasn't there, I guess—a friend who wasn't there; a teacher who wasn't there. You know, somebody just [to] tell you . . . that you were pretty."[9]

Being lonely is painful, sometimes as painful as rejection. Food can be a way to have *something* around you, even if it's not as good as having *someone* around you. Food keeps you busy and your mind occupied, to the point that you don't think you feel the pain, or at least not as fiercely.

Loneliness is also an incredible, if painful, opportunity to

# GOD WANTS TO ASSURE YOU THAT HIS COMPANIONSHIP IS A CONSTANT, ABSOLUTE FACT.

deepen your relationship with God. In His Word He promises to always be with us, so ask Him to make that relationship feel even more real in your life. Ask Him to reveal His love for you. Ask Him how to fill this time and empty space in your heart. He's right there with you, even at this moment, and He wants to assure you that His companionship is a constant, absolute fact. "And surely I am with you always, to the very end of the age" (Matthew 28:20).

## Depression

Feeling blue is a normal point along the spectrum of emotions we all have. That being said, if you're experiencing a depression that keeps hanging on, you need to talk to someone you can trust who can help you get support and treatment. Depression can deepen to the point of seriously interfering with your life. The good news is there's help, be it counseling, medication, or behavior changes. If you think you are experiencing a depression that doesn't seem to be lifting, seek help, because you don't have to feel bad all the time.

If you are feeling slightly blue, try to just sit with the

feeling and truly experience it. When you do this, you lessen the power the feeling has over you, and you won't be as likely to run to the pantry. Try setting a timer for five minutes to do this—just sit still and reflect on your feelings. Or take five minutes and journal. Let your feelings and thoughts spill onto the page, and don't even worry about being coherent or punctuating. Through these activities you may find a real problem that needs to be tackled, or you may discover the feeling will pass, that it's part of a transition you're making in your life. End the five-minute session with a word of thanks to God, even if you don't feel like it. The Bible tells us that praise is a wonderful antidote for the blues.

> *"I have seen his ways, but I will heal him; I will guide him and restore comfort to him, creating praise on the lips of the mourners in Israel. Peace, peace, to those far and near," says the LORD. "And I will heal them."*

> —ISAIAH 57:18–19

> *I will extol the LORD at all times; his praise will always be on my lips.*

> —PSALM 34:1

### Guilt and Shame

These emotions destroy the will to make healthy choices. We just feel so unworthy and unlovely that it's hard to act as if we're anything else. Guilt and shame are often the result of internalizing the messages we hear from the outside world. Someone teases us about our weight, and we agree with them in our hearts. We *are* that awful name they called us.

We don't take the thoughts captive. Instead, we allow them to come into our hearts and minds, and even to bring a friend or two! We don't consider that there is a way out, so we eat to comfort ourselves in our pain and misery.

There's an old saying that I've heard and used many times myself: *Fake it 'til you make it.* It means that after we've spilled our hearts to God

> SOMEONE TEASES US ABOUT OUR WEIGHT, AND WE AGREE WITH THEM IN OUR HEARTS.

about the pain we feel, sometimes we just have to get up off our knees and act as if everything He says about us is true: We *are* loved, worthy, and lovely. "And I pray that you, being rooted and established in love, may have power, together with all the saints, to grasp how wide and long and high and deep is the love of Christ, and to know this love that surpasses knowledge—that you may be filled to the measure of all the fullness of God" (Ephesians 3:17–19).

## Boredom

Who eats out of boredom? Raise your hands! (But don't drop the book please.) Everybody eats out of boredom sometimes, even the really skinny people out there. The best way to stop this behavior is to get out and get going. Leave the room, take a walk, read a book, pray! The key is to be proactive and find an activity that will keep you from grazing.

*Happiness*

Food is associated with celebrations and holidays. Even in the Bible we read about parties and feasts—it was normal then and it's normal now. And because it's normal, it's fine to eat at a celebration. God wants you to enjoy your life and enjoy the party. He gave you the food! Just pay attention to what you're eating and make sure you aren't filling up on junk. Keep these tried-and-true strategies in mind: Eat a snack of fruits and veggies before you go to help take the edge off your hunger. Throughout the party, pay attention to how you're feeling. If you're hungry, eat. If not, don't! Sip on ice water or another low-calorie drink if you need to keep your hands full. Finally, if you aren't sure you have the willpower to stay away from unhealthy food, eat a complete, healthy meal before you go. "He has shown kindness by giving you rain from heaven and crops in their seasons; he provides you with plenty of food and fills your hearts with joy" (Acts 14:17).

## HEALING THE FEELINGS

Did any of those emotional triggers look familiar? Take some time to analyze when, where, and why you eat, and write it all down! Eating over unresolved feelings might be the number one cause of excess weight. And then, the excess weight causes even more unresolved feelings, which leads to more eating, and more weight gain. *Stopping the feel/eat cycle is as important to weight loss as stopping the starve/binge cycle.*

### 1. Identify the feeling.

Getting honest about what you're feeling is a major step to recovery. Whether you use your daily journal or a talk with a friend, learn to play detective with your emotions. Don't judge yourself, but do listen. Ask yourself these four questions:

> **EATING OVER UNRESOLVED FEELINGS MIGHT BE THE NUMBER ONE CAUSE OF EXCESS WEIGHT.**

▼ What is the name of this feeling?

▼ What do I need that I don't feel I am getting?

▼ What does God's Word say?

▼ What should I do to meet this need?

If your Bible has a concordance in the back, which is just a fancy name for an index, try to look up as many verses as you can about the need you are feeling and the emotions you have. You'll be amazed at how practical (and surprising!) God's perspective is when He deals with our emotions.


### 2. Satisfy the real hunger.

When you eat because of an emotional or spiritual hunger, you'll al-ways overeat. You'll never feel full! Have you ever over-eaten and been uncomfortable from all the food in your belly, and yet you still wanted more? That's because your body is telling you the true hunger hasn't been met . . . it's still empty and craving satisfaction. That's what the "detective process" we just talked about is all about. It's not enough to know what you are feeling and why. You have to take action to meet those needs. "As we let go of editing our emotions and valuing them instead, we begin to learn to trust ourselves. We can get off the roller coaster of self-doubt and self-questioning."[10]

Please understand, your cravings for food will fade away when you learn to identify the true hunger and feed it. But if you try and eat to fill those unmet needs, your hunger will never be satisfied and you will have a difficult time losing it for life.

## THE PRAYER JOURNAL'S POWER

Keeping a prayer journal, a tool to help document prayer requests and answers to prayer, is a great way to keep track of your feelings and emotional swings. It's also a handy accountability tool to keep you turning to God with your concerns, hurts, and desires. Take whatever you feel to God. You don't have to edit your feelings, and you don't have to take hours to do this. Just tell God what you feel, because God is ready for you to unload. If you aren't sure how to begin, try this exercise:

▼ Write down what triggered these feelings.
▼ Are you tempted to head to the fridge?
▼ Prayerfully bring the situation to your heavenly Father. Tell Him your needs, your hurts, and what transpired. Ask Him for strength and direction to turn away from the food. Don't forget to give God time to speak to you also.
▼ Write down the outcome of your prayer. How do you feel now?

## 3. Substitute a new behavior for eating.

We are creatures of habit. Part of finding success in healing our feelings is finding new methods of coping with these feelings that act as triggers. There is no end to the list of alternative activities you can consider when you search for new behaviors. Borrow this list[11] or make your own and keep it handy—tape a copy to the fridge if you need to—so you aren't left staring at the fridge when your next trigger begins.

▼ Take a short walk

▼ Turn on some music

▼ Take three deep breaths

▼ Take a bubble bath

▼ Call a friend

▼ Count to 20

▼ Take a short nap

▼ Pray and ask God to help you

▼ Stand up and do some stretches

▼ Go to the bathroom, even if it's only to splash water on your face

▼ Play with your dog

▼ Clean your room

▼ Watch a funny movie

▼ Run up and down the stairs to release tension

▼ Work on a crossword puzzle

▼ Play a video game

## EATING DISORDERS—THE DANGER ZONE

When emotional stress goes for too long without being acknowledged or confessed, it can build up and create a volcano effect that may cause us to feel pressure to make drastic changes that we know aren't healthy, and even things we never thought we would do. But because our feelings are bruised and ignored, we become desperate. Read these three true scenarios that caused teens to turn to eating disorders. Sadly, eating disorders get worse when they're not treated, never better. They can create much bigger problems for you than just losing weight and maintaining a healthy body.

## Those Little Pills

*I started to gain some weight, maybe like fifteen pounds over the last couple of years. It doesn't sound like much, but it really upset me. I hated seeing my body getting bigger, especially my hips. So I tried to throw up, but that was too gross. I couldn't do it very well. Then I did something really stupid: I bought some laxatives.*

*I heard they can help you lose weight, so I've been taking them. It hurts really bad sometimes but I'm starting to feel thinner. The problem is, I can't seem to quit. I am afraid if I stop, I'll get fat. I know it's bad and stupid. But I can't stop, 'cause I would just rather die than be fat! I'm taking almost a whole box of the pills every day now. No one knows about it, but I feel better about myself. At least I haven't gained any more weight.*

## If You Saw Me on the Street . . .

*I know people are thinking, "She'd be so pretty if she lost weight." I started out at a normal weight, but I developed really fast and hated everyone staring at my chest. So I started skipping meals and exercising all the time, and I got very thin. People would say things about me being skinny, but no one ever thought I had a problem.*

But then for some reason I stopped being in control. I started eating one day and couldn't stop. I would just binge when I got home from school and not stop all night. I gained a lot of weight and now my parents are always making comments about my weight. They don't like me being fat.

It's like, being too skinny wasn't their ideal for me, but they really hate me fat. I've never told anyone about my problem with food and weight. I feel like no one knows the real me. If you saw me on the street, you'd think I was a normal, happy teen.

## THE OTHER GIRLS

Whenever I go out with my friends, the other girls get all the attention from the guys. I feel so alone and ugly. I have always had a pretty okay weight because I exercise a lot and am on our school's track team. Last summer I started to eat less and tried to lose weight before school. I did lose fifteen pounds. It made me feel positive and happy.

But then it got harder and harder to not eat, and my weight started to creep back on. I thought if I could just try vomiting, it would help me get back some control. I learned how to do it really well, but now my weight fluctuates. I stuff my face when my parents aren't home and then throw it all up.

It seems like I can control my eating and not eat hardly anything for a while, but then I "have" to binge and eat every sugary thing in the house. And then I throw up. But when I go out with my friends, I get some attention now too. I just pray I'll be able to stop bingeing and vomiting someday.

# LIFE MEANS CHANGE

In all of the stories you just read, the common tragedy is that the girls needed to talk about their experiences and fears but didn't. Food wasn't the core issue; their feelings and thoughts were! And something else: All three of these teens were afraid of their changing bodies and the weight gain that normally accompanies puberty.

Many of the changes in the teen years are not smooth—as you probably know! But did you also know a normal-sized child of ten years of age can expect to double her weight by the time she's sixteen? There can even be a temporary mismatch in height and weight, and it's considered a normal experience, though that doesn't make it feel better. But accepting these changes calmly in a culture that despises fat and worships thin can be scary . . . and extremely difficult.

Yet this is what you have to do: Surrender the fears and hurts and accept that God's plan for you in this time of transition is where the real change needs to begin. Your parents, siblings, and friends all care too, and with their support, you can find peace for this life transition!

"It's not just the biggest losses we try to avoid by eating. It's also the everyday deaths—the disappointments, the illnesses, the rejections, the hurt we feel when life does not turn out the way we'd hoped. Once we realize that we will survive the sadness and hurt, we don't have to deaden ourselves with food. And we can discover that our tender, vulnerable hearts are bigger and more resilient than we ever imagined."[12]

# WHEN TO GET HELP

Sometimes an impulsive decision turns into a lifestyle that's hard to break free from. There are no shortcuts to losing weight for life, or to making peace with the body God has gifted you with. Not laxatives, not skipping meals, not purging, not over-exercising. When you start any of those behaviors, it's not about the weight any longer. It's about a spiritual, emotional, and mental pain that will only bring more hurt.

If you are struggling with an eating disorder, support from friends and family is really important. And if you don't know if your eating behaviors could be called a disorder or not, take a look at this list that Dr. Linda helped me create:

### *You May Have An Eating Disorder If . . .*

▼ you have an intense fear of becoming fat or gaining weight

▼ your menstrual cycles stop or become irregular

▼ you struggle with eating patterns you are powerless to stop

▼ you experience an extreme hatred of your body

▼ you abuse diet pills, laxatives, or illegal drugs to help you lose weight

▼ you binge at least two days a week for a six-month period

▼ you purge after eating, either by vomiting or compulsive exercising

▼ you eat large amounts of food when you are not physically hungry

▼ you eat alone because you are embarrassed by how much you eat

▼ you feel disgusted, guilty, or depressed by the way you eat

If you think you might have an eating disorder, I want to encourage you to tell someone you trust, today. Talk to your parents, or find a teacher you feel comfortable with, and *share your struggle.* Let them guide you to a professional who can help. Wouldn't you like to be free of the pain that is hurting you? Wouldn't you love to be at peace with food and your body? You'll need the support and wisdom of a qualified professional to get there. If you aren't sure what to do, please call 1-800-NEWLIFE to get in touch with a counselor near you who is skilled in treating eating disorders. We want to help you.

~

*Lord, I confess that I eat when I'm feeling something uncomfortable. I need Your help to break free from this cycle. Please nudge me and remind me to play detective, and give me wisdom in knowing what action to take. Give me Your strength to reach for You instead of food. Give me Your power to confess and pour out my heart, instead of shutting it all up and quietly eating instead. Give me a willing heart, a heart willing to feel, and teach me to be willing to sample Your brand of freedom. I love You, Lord. Amen.*

# five

# RELATIONSHIP REHAB

Building Healthy Relationships
to Help You Let Go of Unhealthy Habits

God's original plan was for relationships to be a source of bliss for us. In the creation story of Genesis, God said it *wasn't* good for us to be alone. In that paradise of Eden, where there was no stress or pain, where we could see God eye to eye and ask Him any question we wanted, God gave us one last heavenly gift: intimacy with others. It was the crowning touch to paradise.

The relationships in your life are meant to *bless* you, not curse you. "Well, have you ever met my (insert name here)?" you say. "It's not that simple!"

You're right.

Relationships can be a real mess. People who don't have any relationship skills themselves want to be your friend. Certain people love you, but they don't know how to tell you, or they want to fix you so you'll have a better life. (How helpful.) And there are people who misunderstand you and misjudge you and your motives. Any of these sound familiar? Sometimes all this "relating" makes us want to tune out and numb ourselves with some delicious, comforting food that won't talk back or tell us to clean our rooms. We just want to lounge on the couch and eat and watch TV—the showcase to other people having stressful relationships.

**TV IS POPULAR BECAUSE IT'S AN EASY WAY TO INVITE PEOPLE INTO YOUR HOME WHO WON'T ACTUALLY MESS UP YOUR LIFE.**

TV is popular because it's an easy way to invite people into your home who won't actually mess up your life. The truth is, relationships will probably be the greatest source of pain and stress throughout your life. But with the right skills and approach, relationships can also be the greatest source of encouragement and support to you. "And if one falls down, the other helps" (Ecclesiastes 4:10 MSG).

## WHAT RELATIONSHIPS DO

Relationships are for picking you up when you fall. For the Christian, a relationship is all about lifting you back onto God's path when you're laying on the ground instead of walking His path. Now here's the amazing part: When you follow God's rules for relationships, even the *rotten* people will come through for you. They don't want to, but when they lash out, God can use it to bring a *blessing* into your life instead of the alternative. (Freaky, isn't it?) God can use the worst bullies and loudmouths to bless you and lead you to your dreams, but only if you find the courage to try things His way—which means keeping a tight rein on your thoughts, emotions, and reactions to other people.

Some people in recovery from overeating or abusing food call this part of the program "maintaining their serenity." To stay healthy and keep their triggers at bay, they determine to avoid unnecessary arguments, forgive others quickly, and try to keep petty annoyances in perspective. That's because the stress caused by relationships can be the number one reason people return to unhealthy habits. However, if you follow these principles very closely and are able to stay on the right track and approach relationships day by day, you too, can find freedom.

This next point is really important. *Habitual overeating is a symptom of a soul that is not at rest.* (I know, it's an uncomfortable feeling to realize you aren't at rest, but our mission is to restore to your soul the peace that is yours so that you will seek peace and harmony within your relationships and ultimately find rest.)

Overeating disrupts relationships in many ways. When you feel self-conscious about your body and appearance, you don't want to reach out to others. Perhaps you endured hurtful teasing or the pain of rejection. As a result, you stop reaching out to others, and eventually, the pain you feel from those relationships blocks the dependency you used to have on God. It's easy to blame God when people treat us cruelly. Our natural reaction is to wish God would zap away our problems, but the only way out of this mess does not involve God bringing the entire planet into harmony around your needs by zapping whatever you wish. (Besides, there's *no* way you're cutting in line in front of me if God ever does get in the zapping mood!)

The more you experience how good and right His ways are, the more inclined you are to become dependent on Him in other areas of your life. Perhaps that's a major reason why God won't take your weight problem away just yet. It's more than just the numbers on the scale to Him. It's about the life He can give you if you obey and submit to the uncomfortable process of change and dependence. It's about reaching out when you'd rather stay inside and eat.

## FOUR KEYS TO RELATIONSHIP BUILDING

Improving our relationships with others really consists of working on four biblical actions. When we try to improve our relationships with others, generally there is more harmony and less of the pressure that sends us running to the fridge.

> A recent study shows that teen girls deeply need close-knit friendships, tend to internalize the blame for the friendships if they fail, and look for friends who can be friends with each other.[1]

### 1. Forgive.

God is so sorry for the hurts you have. And even though it might seem like forgiving the person causing your misery is completely unfair, that is exactly what needs to be done. *Even though they might not even care.* The second part of this action is that you also have to forgive God for allowing you to be hurt. We have an example to follow which sets a pretty high standard for us. When Jesus was hanging on the cross,

His prayers reflected a spirit of forgiveness. Imagine how difficult it must have been to pray as He did: "Father, forgive them; they don't know what they're doing" (Luke 23:34 MSG).

Imagine! Jesus forgave the people who were in the process of murdering Him. Those people didn't ask for forgiveness or even care that Jesus forgave them. In fact, they mocked the Lord and hated Him. And yet Jesus forgave them anyway.

Are you willing to forgive the people who hurt you? Are you able to accept that it is not your place or right to inflict punishment or make them regret the way they treated you? Trusting God to forgive these people won't make what they did okay, or mean that God has forgotten the hurt they caused. The love of God is so great, so protective and trustworthy, that you can feel safe in forgiving your enemies.

> Be kind and compassionate to one another, forgiving
> each other, just as in Christ God forgave you.
>
> —EPHESIANS 4:32

## 2. Practice acceptance.

Accept your friends and family as they are without trying to change them. (You can't really expect them to do this if you don't!) Avoid judgments or laughing at their expense. If you become a person who radiates acceptance of others, you will find many friends, and those friendships will become deeper. Acceptance of others helps create humility in yourself. You'll find it easier to stop placing such unrealistic standards on yourself. You'll see that everyone is struggling in some private way. Acceptance of others will also help lessen any shame you feel. Your weight may be a visible problem, but that doesn't mean you're the only one *with* a problem.

To be a Christian means looking to Christ for our example in everything. Our Lord accepted people as they were—sinners, the diseased, the untouchables, even the tax collector! Our task is to model our Lord's behavior each day.

> *Accept one another, then, just as Christ accepted you, in order to bring praise to God.*
>
> —ROMANS 15:7

### 3. Bear with one another.

Some people just drive you crazy, right? Maybe it's your parents nagging you about your weight or your room. Or maybe it's the stuck-up girls at school, or your siblings who bother you night and day. Well, God has directions for how to maintain relationships with these people too—and that doesn't include instructions to merely *tolerate* them. God wants you to *love* them . . . and forgive them over and over, every day.

The reality is you will never have perfect relationships, ever, because there are no perfect people. Here's a little bonus to this step: The better you get at bearing the people who annoy you constantly, the more ready you'll be for true love! That sounds funny, but if you're able to forgive those petty little things people do that bother you, you'll be in training to have a more peaceful marriage. Because when you love someone and spend a lot of time with them, there will *always* be little things that bother you. And that's okay, because your significant other will feel that way about you too.

You want to know my pet peeve? I can't stand to eat while watching TV. I need total silence to listen intently. The problem is that my husband loves to eat while watching TV. And he often chooses

> **YOUR WEIGHT MAY BE A VISIBLE PROBLEM, BUT THAT DOESN'T MEAN YOU'RE THE ONLY ONE *WITH* A PROBLEM.**

healthy snacks, which makes it worse. Have you ever sat next to someone eating Grape-Nuts cereal? I've been tempted to club him with a carrot stick on many occasions. And that, my dears, is true love!

Little faults are just that—little faults. We all have them. By practicing the idea of bearing with someone's little faults, you will bring peace to your relationships.

> *Bear with each other and forgive whatever grievances you may have against one another.*
>
> —COLOSSIANS 3:13

### 4. Trust God to bring people into your life.

Do you think you'll automatically get a boyfriend if you lose weight? Or that people will like you more—that you'll have more friends? Reality check! Although God doesn't appear to

## Four Secrets to Attracting More Friends

1. **Develop interests that can be shared.**

2. **Save your downer moods for established friendships or your parents.**

3. **Don't always look for people who are just like you. They may not have as much to offer as someone who is more unique.**

4. **Give friends your unspoken permission to get close or back away. A wise woman once said, "She holds closest who holds loosest."**

be in the habit of forcing people together, He could bring you into any relationship in the world at any moment. Only God has that power, not the number you see on the scale. You could lose all the weight you needed, maintain a great body, and still be alone. You can't control other people's reactions to you, including whether or not they find you attractive.

So don't put so much pressure on yourself! If you're losing weight to get a guy, you're making demands on your body that your body can't keep. The heart of losing weight should not be a guy. Or a relationship. Or your need for affirmation. Trust that since God can bring you a special relationship at any time, He will bring one when the moment is right.

So instead of running to the fridge when your relationships stress you out, practice these four steps to get your relationships in order. Now let's think about your specific relationships that will change with weight loss. (And no, this doesn't include God—He gets His own chapter!) There are three other primary relationships that are very important to losing weight as a teen which will be radically transformed as you lose weight. They include you and:

▼ your body

▼ food

▼ guys

The first relationship we'll cover is your relationship with your body, which includes how you talk to it. I know, you don't have conversations with your body, or at least not the kind where your body talks

## THE HEART OF LOSING WEIGHT SHOULD NOT BE A GUY

back. Although once when I was getting a massage at a shi-shi spa & resort, the massage "artist" recoiled in horror when he got to my midsection. He apparently believed himself to be some type of natural healer. In a low, dangerous voice, he said my kidneys were "crying out" to him because I was drinking too much coffee. I wanted out of there, fast. I mean, if my kidneys were crying out, who knows what my *thighs* were going to say?

The goal of Lose It For Life isn't just weight loss. It's weight-lessness. Remember, that's the state of mind and heart where you are free of degrading, insulting self-talk about your appearance. "But," you say, "if I stop criticizing myself, won't I lose the motivation to lose weight? If I pretend everything's OK, won't I just quit working at it?"

> ### Seven to One?
>
> **Psychologists say that it takes seven positive comments ... in order to erase one negative comment.[2]**

That's a fair question. But let's put your self-talk to the test, shall we? Let's see how beneficial it is for your weight loss efforts. And hey, if it's working for you, I promise we won't change it. So take this quiz on the facing page and let's see how it's going!

All of the behaviors listed are directly related to your self-talk—what you are saying under your breath, in your mind, and to your heart. And the self-talk that's directed at our bodies is often the most damaging kind we can experience when we're trying to lose weight. When you tell yourself you're fat and the situation is hopeless, you won't have the positive energy to make a healthy choice. But if you remind yourself of the progress being made every day, and that soon you will be that person you've always imagined you could be, you'll have plenty of motivation to reach for an apple instead of a candy bar. Proverbs 23:7 reminds us this is true: "For as he thinks within himself, so he is" (NASB).

Your behavior reflects your feelings, and where do your feelings get started? Not in your *heart*—no, they start in your

# IS YOUR SELF-TALK WORKING?

When I eat too much, I want to get
back on track right away.          True/False

When I see myself in a mirror, I smile.   True/False

When a friend tells me I look good,
I accept the compliment gracefully.   True/False

When I've had a bad day, I look
forward to my workouts—not food.   True/False

When I work out, I feel refreshed
and peaceful.          True/False

When everyone else is pigging out,
I feel proud of myself for saying no.   True/False

When I get hungry, I know I'll reach
for healthy foods.          True/False

When a social activity is coming up,
I get excited about the possibilities.   True/False

*head!* Whatever you think about yourself is ultimately what you'll become. A friend used to tell me, "Your expectations *will* be met."

Here's an example from real life: When you go to a horror show (my favorite kind!), do you feel light and happy, or do you scrunch down in your seat and hold your breath? See, even though you intellectually understand that the movie isn't real, just the fact that you're willing to entertain those thoughts is enough to get your blood pumping and your nerves rattled. That's why you feel afraid at the movies, even though you know the psycho killer is onscreen, rather than in the movie theater. You're willing to entertain the possibility that the killer is really whacking away up there, which makes your feelings go wild and your pulse shoot through the roof.

So, *intellectually* you may believe you're a great person inside and out, but if you briefly entertain ugly thoughts about yourself, you could potentially set in motion a cascade of reactions and behaviors. Even as you tell yourself you "know" what a nice person you are, you could be punishing yourself with too much food. Self-talk, those little whispers we make to our hearts, has the potential to lift us up or break us down. It is a power we can, and must, harness.

But before we can harness the power of self-talk, we've got to know exactly what is being said. Take this quiz to uncover your most common self-talk . . . and be honest!

## What'd You Say?

1. When I step on the scale, my first thought is:

_____

_____

_____

2. When I see myself in a picture, I think:

_____

_____

_____

3. When friends ask me to go swimming, I:

_____

_____

_____

4. When I am shopping for clothes, I worry that:

_____

_____

_____

5. When I have to choose between unhealthy and healthy foods, I think:

_____

_____

_____

If your self-talk isn't transitioning to a more positive line, it's time to address that matter! And guess who has the best answer?

## God's Exchange Policy (no receipt needed)

God intends for you to be free and weightless, and He has a specific plan for helping you manage self-talk. We've already discussed how to take a thought captive. Now let's talk about what to replace it with. Here's God's exchange policy from Philippians 4:8:

> Summing it all up, friends, I'd say you'll do best by filling your minds and meditating on things true, noble, reputable, authentic, compelling, gracious—the best, not the worst; the beautiful, not the ugly; things to praise, not things to curse (MSG).

We are to replace every negative thought with another that is true and authentic and gracious. It doesn't matter if you don't believe it at first. If you really want to lose weight forever and experience how divine weightlessness can be, you have to begin by extending God's gracious love to yourself.

Put it another way. Whom would you rather work for: a boss that calls you names and makes fun of you, or someone who sees the best in you, no matter what? If you worked for someone who loved you and complimented you every day, wouldn't you be motivated to live up to their expectations? It makes sense, doesn't it? Now you're getting the picture!

## NOW YOU'RE TALKING!

Using the advice in Philippians, let's make a list of three statements we can repeat daily until they become the self-talk we always use.

1. The most beautiful part of my appearance is:

_____

_____

_____

2. I can praise God for my appearance because:

_____

_____

_____

3. As I try to lose weight, I am most proud of myself so far for:

_____

_____

_____

_____

I can sense your skepticism. Repeating these statements every day sounds like an ineffective activity, doesn't it? I mean, how can some simple words really change anything? Truly, you'll be surprised at the difference in your perspective if you faithfully take each negative personal thought captive and replace it with an alternative from this list. It reminds me of a story I once heard about a doctor.

His patient was a man who had so much stress and unhappiness that his body was breaking down from carrying the load. The man suffered indigestion, insomnia, headaches, and aches and pains. The doctor took out his prescription pad and wrote the man the most powerful prescription he could and instructed his patient to fill it right away. It was very important to follow the directions exactly as he was ordered, the doctor emphasized, because the medicine would work wonders.

So of course, this guy shoots out of the doctor's office really anxious to fill this prescription and get back his life. And when he unfolded the paper and got a good look at it, what do you think it was? You got it, a prescription for "self-talk." Specifically, the doctor had given him a prescription to read and repeat several Bible verses three times each day. Of course, the guy got so angry he nearly keeled over right then, but he decided later to try the doctor's advice. Much to his surprise, it *worked*. Peace came back into his life, his physical problems melted away, and he was able to live the life he wanted.

Now, here's a prescription for you: Repeat these verses several times a day and see how much better you feel in a month:

▼ "I praise you because I am fearfully and wonderfully made; your works are wonderful, I know that full well. My frame was not hidden from you when I was made in the secret place" (Psalm 139:14–15).

▼ "So if the Son sets you free, you are free through and through" (John 8:36 MSG).

## FRIENDSHIP WITH FOOD

The changes you'll experience in the Lose It For Life program will gradually help you to use food for fuel, not friendship. That's a radical change for a lot of us! Food has been such a safe and comforting ally, a spot of comfort in a very difficult world. And no one can give that up until they've built bridges to God and then to other people in order to have the supportive relationships in place that feed a hungry heart and spirit. Opening doors to relationships with the keys we talked about a little earlier are necessary in order to begin letting go of food.

While the number of boys who say they "have confidence in themselves" remains relatively stable through adolescence, the numbers for girls drop steadily from 72 percent in sixth grade to only 55 percent in tenth grade.[3]

It's not a one-time decision, either, and it won't mean overnight deliverance. You can't force yourself or berate yourself. Truly, it's a matter of trust. You have to grow emotionally and spiritually into a place where you can trust that your needs will be met so that you stop trying to meet the needs yourself. The following story, retold from the book, *Sleeping with Bread*, by Dennis, Sheila, and Matthew Linn, demonstrates this principle.

> *During World War II, a group of war orphans was gathered together in order to protect them from further harm. For the first time since the horrors of the war began, the children were given daily food and shelter. Finally, all their needs were being met. Yet at night, the children were restless and frightened—they couldn't sleep. Though their minds could see they were safe and their needs were being met, the information wasn't going any farther. They were too young to understand that they must trust their caretakers to continue to provide. But because the orphans weren't able to let this information sink into their hearts, they couldn't let themselves trust.*
>
> *Eventually, one caregiver got an idea straight from heaven. He let each child take a piece of bread to bed with them after they had finished eating their dinners. The children were told that they could hold the bread all night. If they ate their slice, someone would bring them another. That night, and every night after, the children slept soundly. No one was afraid any more, and trust was finally something they could do, because they had something to hold on to. There was proof very close to them that their needs would be met. Literally, they didn't go to bed empty-handed! They slept while holding onto a promise.*

Now, it would be counter-productive for us to go to bed holding a piece of bread, but we can use the same principle.

We have to know our needs will be met before we can let go of our fears and disruptive behaviors. So how do we let go of food and embrace God's provision? Here are three simple ways:

*Say a little goodbye every day.* Ask God to give you one clear chance each day to see how you use food to comfort yourself. And ask for His divine blessing on that moment; pray that He would give you the strength and peace to let go, to say goodbye to the hold food has over you, just for today.

> But this happened that we might not rely on ourselves but on God. . . . On him we have set our hope that he will continue to deliver us.
>
> 2 CORINTHIANS 1:9–10

*Take a small step of trust each day.* Ask God also to show you plainly one example each day of how you can put all your trust in Him, even if it is just regarding one small decision. Be waiting for that moment and let God show you His love right then.

> "Test me in this," says the LORD Almighty, "and see if I will not throw open the floodgates of heaven and pour out so much blessing that you will not have room enough for it."
>
> —MALACHI 3:10

*Find a verse that reassures you every day.* Every morning, spend a few minutes looking up verses that encourage you to trust God and let go of destructive behaviors. God promises that His Word can actually penetrate and transform you when you read it. Take that promise and make it your own!

*For the word of God is living and active.*

—HEBREWS 4:12

God can set you free from trusting in food. He will deliver you from life's difficult moments, but only if you're willing to trust Him instead. The biggest battle you face is not doing it, but *making the decision* to do it. God will give you the strength and the heart to face your fears and move into the new life He has planned for you. You don't have to fight the battle; you just have to keep making a decision to turn to God when the battle hits.

> YOU DON'T HAVE TO FIGHT THE BATTLE; YOU JUST HAVE TO KEEP MAKING A DECISION TO TURN TO GOD WHEN THE BATTLE HITS.

And remember, God wants you to be in relationships with others. He wants you to be surrounded by people who reflect back to you His love and unconditional acceptance. He will *give* you the ability to let go of food and reach out to a friend, if you can make the decision to trust Him first when fears arise.

Developing friendships and peer support is a great way to lessen the pain of saying goodbye to food as a friend. Experts say:

▼ Women tend to lose weight in groups, while men tend to lose weight on their own.[4]

▼ People who use the buddy system when losing weight lose twice as much weight as those who don't.[5]

▼ Low peer support increases your risk for binge eating.[6]

▼ One of the strongest factors associated with whether or not you are physically active is the support you receive in relationships.[7]

There's no doubt about this fact; healthy relationships can help you reach a healthy weight. Saying goodbye to food as a source of comfort and companionship opens the door for the real sources of comfort and companionship—good friends!

## LOVE HANDLES AND YOUR LOVE LIFE

If America were like that little tropical island I referenced in the beginning of this book, where teen girls were supposed to be as big as possible to be beautiful, would you be reading this book right now? (Nope.) If everyone loved teens who were very, very heavy, and thin girls just couldn't get a date, would you even care about losing weight? (I doubt it. But isn't it fun to imagine turning the tables like that?)

Most experts agree that adults are more likely to want to lose weight for health reasons while teens are more likely to want to lose weight for social reasons—especially dating.

Girls who struggle with their weight are more likely to be teased and bullied, and less likely to date.[8]

First, though the pressure to lose weight in order to get a guy is not very healthy, it's everywhere. A study of magazine covers showed that weight loss articles are often placed next to articles on how to attract a guy or dating advice.[9] The magazine message is clear: If you want romance, you'd better be thin. Of course, not all of America is getting the message. The next time you're in public, note how many adults are overweight and how many marriages and babies you see. Clearly, not everyone is a size six, yet romance is still alive! I guess the guys aren't reading our magazines.

But teens do tend to put more emphasis on their weight, especially girls. Consider this finding in a recent study: "Although overweight boys are dissatisfied with their dating lives, they still report dating more often than overweight girls."[10] If the guys were telling the truth—and this is a *big* if!—it means guys who

> **THE MAGAZINE MESSAGE IS CLEAR: IF YOU WANT ROMANCE, YOU'D BETTER BE THIN.**

know they are overweight can still get dates. It's different for girls, isn't it? There's just a harsher standard for females, and this issue definitely continues into adulthood.

You *are* going to be judged by your weight. I hate it because it's not fair. What you weigh isn't a true measure of who you are. Thankfully, that's *not* the only deciding vote. In the long run, the right people will care more about how you *make them feel* rather than what you look like. One study proved that when we associate people with positive feelings, we view them as being much more attractive than they actually are. In this study, pictures of heavy people were shown to subjects who had to rank the pictured people's attractiveness. Next, the researchers told the study participants that the people were very kind, or generous, or anything else positive they could think of. Guess what happened? That's right—the study participants decided these strangers were actually much better looking than they had originally thought. That's the first key to unlocking the doors to a healthier dating life: *Realize it's not always about your weight . . . it's about how you make people feel.*

As you lose weight, you will probably see a difference in your love life. We've talked about the difference between diets and Lose It For Life before, but it's especially important with this topic. Diets can spell disaster for your relationships because diets only change the way you eat, and only for a short time. You don't pick up any relationship skills munching on raw broccoli florets—am I right? With weight loss should come a plan that gives you new ways to relate to people. Dramatic weight loss brings change into your relationships, and will probably cause you to attract more attention from guys. You will need to know how to handle that.

Using the principles in this book is not only critical for

Having a boyfriend isn't all about your looks. Hopefully the guy you are interested in has enough of his own insecurities and fears without being too wrapped up in yours as well. And for all the guys I interviewed while writing this book, here is the message they want girls to hear:

### *Please, puh-lease, stop saying, "I'm so fat."*

Put yourself in their place . . . they are going crazy from this, and no wonder. What can any guy say that will possibly make any difference? If he says nothing, you think he's insensitive. If he agrees, you dump him. If he says something neutral, like, "You're not fat; you're propor-tionate," they you would probably *still* dump him. Guys know they can't win when they hear you saying this dreaded phrase. So stop putting them in a difficult position.

long-term weight loss, it can make all the difference in having a happy, balanced dating life as well. Let me explain. With Lose It For Life, you possess:

▼ tools to form a new dependence on God and to trust His plan

▼ positive suggestions for how to improve your feelings,

and self-talk, which can have a big impact on your outlook

▼ new confidence that springs from both your improved relationship with God and your accomplishment in losing weight

▼ a new respect for your own boundaries

Did you catch that word "boundaries"? That's right, losing weight on this plan means learning to respect your own God-given boundaries for your body, which has an *enormous* impact on your dating life. When you numb yourself with food, you're ignoring the signals from your body and spirit that you've had too much and need to stop. You're forcing yourself to do something, that, in your heart, you know isn't right or healthy. You feel powerless to stop, and depression sets in. You feel shame as you trap yourself in a pattern you don't like.

Bad romantic relationships and overeating share a close connection. They both involve a pattern of numbing yourself to what you really feel and need as you try to force something good out of a rotten deal. When you begin to learn to trust your boundaries, however, and to respect and protect them, you develop the inner strength to both *know* the right thing to do and also the will to *do* it. That life skill can help you in the dating world more than any other tip I can share.

It's a principle you'll have to live out for a while to really appreciate. You may find that by working through these issues with food, you're able to have better relationships than you ever could have had without the struggle with your weight. You'll recognize unhealthy habits and relationships before you've spent years of your life with them.

If you are scared about attracting attention because of past trauma or abuse, this is a major roadblock to recovery that you'll need a good counselor to work through. It's not something I can treat lightly in a book or give you a few quick tips to deal with. Please, if you've been wounded by abuse in the past, especially sexual abuse, you need to know that losing weight may open up those old hurts and make you believe you will always be stuck with food. In truth, this is a normal, natural defense to protect yourself, so don't beat yourself up for coping in the only way you knew how. Just try to find a qualified counselor who can show you how to cope and how to heal. If you aren't sure how to start or where to turn, call 1-800-NEWLIFE. This organization has a list of counselors available in your area who are ready to help.

Losing weight the healthy way will impact your relationships. No doubt about it. As you begin to feel good about yourself, you are more likely to invest in making people feel good about themselves too. God wants you to embrace your life, and all the people He has put in it . . . and that's our prayer for you too!

*Lord, my relationships may need as much work as my eating habits. And it seems they are so closely entwined: I eat when I'm lonely, and when I want to reach out, I'm embarrassed about my weight. And I'm afraid no one will love me if I don't lose weight. What I need right now is the deep, real reassurance that can only come from You. Show me that I am deeply, truly loved and secure. You are the friend who will never leave, never judge, and always comfort. I will learn to love others as I experience how You love me. Thank You for Your constant guidance. Please lead me to people who will speak Your words into my life. Show me Your love at work here on earth. Amen.*

# six
# WILL GOD HELP ME LOSE WEIGHT?

### Nurturing Your Spiritual Life
### so You Can Slim Down in Your Physical Life

Have you ever wondered what God thinks about weight? Or whether He will do anything to help fix the problem, or answer the desperate prayers we say? Well, the Ten Commandments don't say a lot about saturated fats or cellulite, and the back of my Bible has a lot of maps, but no BMI charts. So, now what?

### *Does God care?*

*Is there a "right" weight for me that pleases Him?*

*What will He do for me to help me win this struggle?*

## FOUR DOORS TO GOD'S POWER

God's Word says: "Unless the LORD builds the house, its builders labor in vain. Unless the LORD watches over the city, the watchmen stand guard in vain" (Psalm 127:1).

Americans do a lot of things to lose weight. We try a lot of diets and start a lot of exercise programs . . . and we've read

# WHAT WE WANT OUT OF THE "THIN LIFE" ISN'T ABOUT OUR SIZE.

the stats on how well we're doing trying to lose weight on our own! One of the reasons Americans are failing at their weight loss efforts is that they are attempting to "build their houses" without God. We need God's help to lose weight because we want to do more than just lose weight. We want to be filled up in our spirits and hearts. The hunger that drives many of us to overeat can't be satisfied by food. And what we want out of the "thin life" isn't about our size. Nope. It's about the happiness we imagine goes along with living thin.

God *wants* us to experience that happiness. But He's not going to wait until we're "perfect" or thin before we start to experience the good life. He wants to start blessing you right now, today, before you've even lost one single pound. He wants to do for you what you cannot do for yourself. But in order for God to do this, we need to give God a building permit to work.

### Accept Reality

God wants us to call out to Him in our need, but first we have to be willing to accept that we *are* needy. Accepting the reality of our situation is a tough first hurdle. It means accepting the truth about our circumstances and confronting the lies our culture whispers to us. Acceptance means agreeing that:

▼ No one else caused your problem and no one else is going to fix it for you.

▼ Changing will require painful moments.

▼ You'll never achieve perfection, but you *can* achieve self-acceptance.

We can make a lot of excuses before we begin to accept the truth about our situation and our limitations. We blame others—"My parents nagged me all the time about my weight. I wasn't fat then, but now I really do have a problem. They messed me up." And although parents can certainly play a role in how a person views weight, blame doesn't get you very far. Maybe this isn't the path you would have chosen for your life, but God can do incredible things through it. And accepting your reality, without blame and without excuses, prepares you to receive God's grace. It opens your eyes so that you can witness God working. It wipes the slate clean so that God can spell out His own will. Forgiveness is the best antidote to blame.

And lastly, acceptance frees you from pursuing a worldly ideal that was never meant for you (or most women!). When God designed you, no detail was overlooked. There is a weight range at which your whole body functions at its best, and that's the weight God wants you to find. It's about finding *freedom* by focusing on what God wants for you rather than on what you think you want, whether it's our society's approval or a boyfriend or to be "happy" because you're thin at last. The world would have you get to a weight that makes you look "good"—even if it may do damage to your overall health. Ladies, that's enslavement, not God's best for your life.

### Surrender

Surrender acknowledges God's existence and His place in your life. If you want to get off the weight loss roller coaster,

## REALITY CHECK

then surrender to God's way of doing things. You have to accept that He is in the driver's seat and you are merely along for the ride. And let's be truthful—has your way worked out like you hoped? No. But His grace is sufficient, and He can bring healing! Surrender brings about the fulfillment of God's promise in Jeremiah 29:14: "'I will be found by you,' declares the LORD, 'and will bring you back from captivity.'"

Face it, if you could have lost the weight by yourself, you would have. But you didn't, because God is ready to change more than just your size. God wants to give you a different life: "If you grasp and cling to life on your terms, you'll lose it, but if you let that life go, you'll get life on God's terms" (Luke 17:33 MSG). Surrender means letting go of the control of:

*My own agenda:*

▼ how fast I lose weight

▼ how much weight I lose

- ▼ my ideal, final shape and weight
- ▼ all of my plans for my "perfect" body

*My relationships:*

- ▼ how people treat me and react to my new habits
- ▼ whether I get a boyfriend when I lose weight
- ▼ if people accept or reject me

*My "secret self":*

- ▼ where I go for comfort
- ▼ how I blow off steam
- ▼ the person I want to become when I lose weight

God also wants us to *surrender* the burdens we are not meant to carry. Surrender doesn't mean you stop trying, only that you stop trying to run the show. Surrendering to God on a daily, hourly, and moment-by-moment basis will humble you, but it will also free you from overwhelming pressure and stress. Can we make it without surrender? Listen to Jesus reply to the same question: "'No chance at all,' Jesus said, 'if you think you can pull it off by yourself. Every chance in the world if you trust God to do it'" (Luke 18:27 MSG).

### Take Responsibility

Your weight is merely a reflection of your habits. When Wynona Judd went public on Oprah about her private battle with her weight, her sister Ashley made a comment that highlighted this principle. She said she knew her sister wasn't

# CAN WE MAKE IT WITHOUT SURRENDER? NO CHANCE AT ALL.

eating healthy foods, because healthy foods couldn't create and support a weight like Wynona's. That really impressed on me the fact that what we like to think is a private habit is really a public battle. When we're struggling with our weight, it's pretty obvious that our struggle is not in cutting back on lettuce and carrots, right? (I would be a happy woman if I ever craved them the way I crave chocolate!)

Only *you* can change your private habits. That means you'll be the one dragging yourself to the gym, or saying no to another helping of dessert, or finding time to write in your journal. I know many of us dream of just turning ourselves over to some celebrity chef and trainer that would allow us to emerge six weeks later with a new body. Shows like *Extreme Makeover* fuel that fantasy.

But if someone else could lose weight for you and change you the way they wanted to, they would make you over in *their* ideal image. You would automatically forfeit some of the blessings God has in mind for you. Taking responsibility gives you the *gift* of saying no. It makes sense, right? This is your body, and the prize (a thinner you) is yours alone, which means the work is going to mainly fall on you. See this journey exactly as it is—a wonderful opportunity to do something really great for you.

*May all the gifts and benefits that come from God our Father, and the Master, Jesus Christ, be yours.*

—1 CORINTHIANS 1:3 (MSG)

*Invest Time*

Plan to invest at least thirty minutes a day writing in your journal, reading through this book, and most importantly, studying Scriptures and praying and listening to God. Eventually this time spent with God will become the source of your constant, renewing strength to keep making positive changes. What you are attempting to do is very difficult—in fact many adults never do it successfully.

By spending time with God, you can ask Him to do for you what's impossible for you to do on your own, because He will carry your burdens. You can ask Him to fill your need for love and acceptance. You can ask Him for the peace that makes bingeing a distant memory. Ask, because God will answer you in surprising, delightful ways. You'll need this special time with God every day so you can begin to understand how He works, and what He might ask of you, and what He might want to give you. Make your "quiet time" a part of your new lifestyle that doesn't change, even when your body's shape does. And as you let go of your own agenda and begin to walk with God through this problem, He will stand by you and work a mighty transformation!

## WHAT GOD WILL DO

God's Word is filled with promises about how He will transform your life and deliver you from unhealthy habits. As you are freed from your struggle against overeating, turn to these Scriptures and meditate on how God will:

▼ give you freedom from the power of sin (Romans 6:22)

▼ provide the tools to demolish strongholds (2 Corinthians 10:4)

▼ arm you with strength to face the battle (Psalm 18:32)

▼ keep you on the right track (Proverbs 3:8)

▼ give you self-control (Galatians 5:22–23)

▼ continuously move you in the right direction (Philippians 1:6)

▼ work in you to do His will and act in accord with His purpose (Philippians 2:13)

▼ make you a new person (2 Corinthians 5:17)

The key is to spend time every day reading and meditating on His Word. Let God fill you with His promises every day and you'll be well-prepared to face the pressures of the day. And if you are a newcomer to reading the Scriptures and aren't sure where or how to begin, start with those verses listed above. For each verse, ask yourself,

▼ *What* does this verse say?

▼ *How* does it apply to my life?

▼ Pray for God to reveal His thoughts to you for the day ahead.

Even a few minutes' time invested in your faith life each day will reap great benefits. Reading God's promises for ten minutes each morning just might help you say no to an extra helping somewhere in the day, which means you've just saved an hour or more of guilt and shame, and possibly even avoided an "Oh, well, I've blown it now" binge.

*Trust GOD from the bottom of your heart;*
*don't try to figure out everything on your own.*
*Listen for GOD's voice in everything you do,*
*everywhere you go;*

*he's the one who will keep you on track.*
*Don't assume that you know it all.*
*Run to GOD! Run from evil!*
*Your body will glow with health,*
*your very bones will vibrate with life!*

—PROVERBS 3:5–8 (MSG)

## THE PROMISE THAT CHANGES IT ALL

Most diets are based on the premise that you'll be worth loving once you lose weight. (That's why the diet articles are next to get-the-guy articles!) We diet because we want to be loved. Yet the Bible says something very different in Romans 8:38–39:

> *For I am convinced that neither death nor life, neither angels nor demons, neither the present nor the future, nor any powers, neither height nor depth, nor anything else in all creation, will be able to separate us from the love of God that is in Christ Jesus our Lord.*

### THIS IS HOW I THINK THAT VERSE APPLIES TO US:

> *For I am convinced that neither size 4 nor size 14,*
> *neither sugar nor fat, neither binge nor starve, nor any*
> *exercise plan or rebellious streak, nor anything else at the gym, in*
> *the mirror, or in my fridge, will be able to separate me from God's*
> *love. There is no size He will love me more at than where I am*
> *today. I'll never lose even one pound that makes Him love me*
> *more, nor grow so big*
> *that He cares for me any less.*

God's love is the most powerful supernatural force on earth. It surrounds you at every moment—when you are eating too much or too little, weeping or laughing, sleeping or playing. You can't run from God. God won't yell at you or call you names for messing up. God always works to give us His best, even when we're in a mess we created ourselves.

Your mistakes don't separate you from God, and you should view them as they are: opportunities to draw closer to Him. You don't have to be strong or have iron willpower to lose weight God's way. It's okay to be weak, and it's okay when you make a mistake, because God will help you get back on a healthy track. He wants you to live a life of freedom rather than one in which you are enslaved to food or diets. It's a radical way of living called "weightlessness" that God has in mind for you! He will go to great lengths to set you free from your self-imposed prison. So you must learn to trust Him with your mistakes, and not just your good days.

> You're famous for helping; God, give us a break.
> Your reputation is on the line.
> Pull us out of this mess, forgive us our sins—
> do what you're famous for doing!
>
> —PSALM 79:9 (MSG)

When you make your weight loss journey a story about you and God, incredible things can happen. Suddenly, it's not just you versus the scale. It's all about having someone near who will not only catch you when you fall, but carry you back to a safe place. God loves you through these battles! First Corinthians 13:4–7 tells us exactly how He cares for us:

Love never gives up. Love cares more for others than for self. Love doesn't want what it doesn't have. Love doesn't strut, *doesn't have a swelled head, doesn't force itself on others, isn't always "me first," doesn't fly off the handle, doesn't keep score of the sins of others, doesn't revel when others grovel, takes pleasure in the flowering of truth, puts up with anything, trusts God always, always looks for the best, never looks back, but keeps going to the end (MSG).*

God doesn't keep track of your mistakes. He "never looks back" and will keep "going [with you] to the end."

## WHAT TO DO WHEN GOD SAYS " "

Has God ever said " " to you? He's said that many times to me, and it just makes me crazy.

We can pour our hearts out to Him, and wait in eager anticipation, only to hear the dreaded " ." It sounds like silence, although I am sure God is communicating on some level we can't hear. So what are we to do when God seems to fall silent?

The Bible has some specific, if mysterious, instructions: *Keep asking.*

Personally, it drives me batty when someone keeps repeating the same question over and over. However, this is God's board game, so we'll play by His rules. Jesus told us the story of the persistent widow in Luke 18:1–8 to demonstrate to us the power of patiently asking and asking again and even again:

*Jesus told his disciples a story about how they should keep on praying and never give up: In a town there was once a judge who didn't fear God or care about people. In that same town there was a widow who kept going to the judge and saying,*

*"Make sure that I get fair treatment in court."*

*For a while the judge refused to do anything. Finally, he said to himself, "Even though I don't fear God or care about people, I will help this widow because she keeps on bothering me. If I don't help her, she will wear me out."*

*The Lord said: Think about what that crooked judge said. Won't God protect his chosen ones who pray to him day and night? Won't he be concerned for them? He will surely hurry and help them. But when the Son of Man comes, will he find on this earth anyone with faith?* (CEV).

I don't know all of the spiritual forces at work when we pray, or why sometimes we seem to hear static or even complete silence. But God clearly wants us to *keep asking.* And that's good news for those of us who struggle with our weight and eating, because it's not a habit we can give up forever, is it? We have to eat several times a day, and we're going to be prone to make mistakes. But let's be persistent in asking God's help and blessing on our efforts. I find myself praying almost every day for a willing spirit, and for a desire to eat natural, healthy foods. I ask God not to give up on me, but to keep working in my life, changing and uprooting whatever needs to go, and setting me free to be the person He had in mind when He created me. Keep asking!

## How to Handle Temptation

God loves us more than we can imagine, but that doesn't mean He'll isolate us from the real world. And the real world has plenty of temptations, doesn't it? You're home in an empty house, by yourself. The fridge is packed with left-overs from a party: cookies, cake, chips, dips, buffalo wings,

Have you ever felt the embarrassment of knowing you have the power of a living God at work in your life, and yet you aren't able to keep from overeating? Christian teens who struggle with their weight often feel the weight of this extra guilt too. For instance, how many times have you read or heard this passage of Scripture: "Do you not know that your body is a temple of the Holy Spirit, who is in you, whom you have received from God? You are not your own; you were bought at a price. Therefore honor God with your body" (1 Corinthians 6:19–20)?

I can feel so guilty sometimes when that verse is read, because I do know I have a responsibility to maintain this temple for God. (You'd think God would want a big one, though!) But seriously, if you have ever struggled with this same guilt, let me assure you of some very distinct truths. First, the temple is a place that should facilitate worship of God, not preoccupation of self. And we are commanded to honor God with our bodies, but honor actually starts with trust. First, we learn how to trust God and His ways, and this, in turn, creates honor. So it's not about creating a buff body to present to God as a tribute; it's about trusting God with our bodies and bringing Him honor by giving Him what we have, as it is. You don't have to be perfect just because you know a perfect God. And remember: This is His temple. So let Him have it, every room, every space, every inch. It's not about you. Got guilt? Let go, and let God in.

and soda. And to make matters worse, you've had a lousy day. You're tense and tired, and the last thing you want to do is eat healthy food. You want to enjoy all the goodies and enjoy some solitude. Friend, you're being tempted, but you have a lot of options! There's more than one way to deal with tempting food . . . and this is not a binge-and-then-get-back-on-the-wagon type of diet! So let's look at your options.

▼ If you're hungry, go ahead and include a small bit of the enticing junk food in your balanced dinner. You don't have to say no to everything all the time. Keeping the junk to a minimum in an otherwise balanced meal means you *can* have any food—and it won't all land on your hips.

▼ If you're not hungry yet, tell yourself you'll indulge a little when you do finally get hungry. This short-circuits the rebellious streak in all of us. When we know something is not forbidden, it often loses its hold on us! This principle has worked wonders for me. I've had a chocolate-praline fudge cake in my house all week and I've had perhaps two small slices. I know I can eat it if I want, although only after I've eaten my quota of veggies and fruits each day, but honestly, it hasn't been calling my name. If I had told myself it was strictly off-limits, however, I'm sure I'd be typing with one hand right now and stuffing cake in my mouth with the other!

But what about the other temptation, the kind that grabs your mind and doesn't seem to let go? The kind of temptation you feel powerless to stop, and powerless to stop yourself from giving in to? Well, God has a specific plan for dealing with those moments in 1 Corinthians 10:13:

*No temptation has seized you except what is common to man. And God is faithful; he will not let you be tempted beyond what you can bear. But when you are tempted, he will also provide a way out so that you can stand up under it.*

Let's review what this verse says. First, God tells you that this temptation is a very common one, so you shouldn't feel ashamed or weird. You can pick up the phone and

## GOD WILL PROVIDE AN ESCAPE.

tell a friend what you're experiencing, and chances are very good that they'll understand. And just knowing you are not alone, and that someone else has probably experienced the very same feeling, is a powerful antidote to the pressure temptation brings—the way it makes you feel like no one else is tempted like you are.

God also won't let the temptation overwhelm you. He promises you will always have more strength in Him than weakness to give in. If you know you're on the winning team, you're not as frightened of the opponent.

God will provide an escape. Pray that God will make your escape routes very easy to spot. Maybe the phone will ring, or the dog will swipe the snack, or you'll catch a glimpse of a clothing sale ad in the paper. If your house has doors, that's likely the easiest escape you can take. Keep your running shoes near the door for a quick escape when you need it. Other good options include a quick temple and forehead massage, chewing a piece of sugarless gum, or turning on some music to distract yourself. If you can visualize how you'll defeat the temptation, you can go on autopilot when the urge hits and safely glide on out of there. Don't forget: You're not alone . . . God won't let you go under. God will provide an escape.

## THE PRAYER GOD *WON'T* ANSWER

"Why can't God just take this weight away for me?" Isn't that a question you've asked a million times? Is there a reason why God makes us fight this battle every day in the trenches, instead of just granting us a new body? In James 4:2–3 we learn what may be keeping us from this very thing: "You want something but don't get it. You kill and covet, but you cannot have what you want. You quarrel and fight. You do not have, because you do not ask God. When you ask, you do not receive, because you ask with wrong motives, that you may spend what you get on your pleasures."

**GOD IS A POWERFUL ALLY IN THIS BATTLE, NOT BECAUSE HE VALUES THINNESS, BUT BECAUSE HE WANTS YOUR UNDIVIDED ATTENTION!**

God will never give you the answer to your prayer if it replaces Him in your heart and life. Because God is good, He can only give you things that bless your life and cause you to hunger for Him. If you are losing weight because you want to be like people and pop stars who dress or act in immoral ways, God is *not* going to answer that prayer. If having a great body is the passport you need before you can live out a destructive lifestyle, God's not going to process the paperwork.

The irony is, God cares more about your weight than you do, because He knows what it is robbing you of. If you spend so much time obsessing about it, you're going to miss His gifts and miracles.

God can also work miracles through your current weight, which:

▼ keeps you humble, a quality that pleases God and allows Him to bless you more

▼ makes you focus on God and His power instead of your own

▼ develops in you compassion for others who don't fit in or measure up

▼ opens your spiritual eyes as you make choices every day based on faith and trust instead of quick fixes and instant cures

You might want to get *fit* to have a better *shape* . . . but God will use your struggle with your weight to *shape* you into a woman *fit* to change the world. And that's not a bad trade-off!

If I asked you how much Madam Curie weighed, or if Mother Teresa had cellulite, would you know? Would you care? In a hundred years, no one will be sitting around talking about how great your stomach looked in a cutaway tank top, but they might still be talking about the things you accomplished and the lives you changed. Aim for a great legacy, not just a great body!

# What to Do When You Want to Give Up

Fighting a problem with weight can be exhausting, especially when you're making big changes in your whole life and not just around your eating habits. There will be days when your progress seems too small—or nonexistent!—for all the effort you're making. (In my experience, that's usually right before a big breakthrough!) But when you're tempted to give up and give in, consider what Jennifer Cecil, a weight loss counselor with Lose It For Life says:

---

### Weight Loss and the "Warrior Spirit"[2]
### By Jennifer Cecil, M.Ed., CPC

*Sometimes I am tempted to stop trying, to accept myself at this weight, to give up the goal . . .*

*Something rises up inside. I call it the "warrior spirit," the part of me that wants to WIN, The part of me that wants to OVERCOME and DEFEAT the enemy. If I am in a battle, I do not want to lose. If my addiction to food is something that the enemy of my soul uses to diminish my destiny, I DO NOT WANT TO ALLOW IT! I want to try again. I NEVER want to give up! I will NOT concede. I will keep trying until the day that I die. After all, I have the same power in me that raised Jesus from the dead. How can I NOT have victory in this battle?*

---

When you struggle with your weight loss journey, turn back to this page and go through these six reasons why you should keep on struggling, *even if you don't feel like it!* Sometimes you have to behave as if you want to in order to get your body to come willingly. If we consider Jennifer's comments, this is what we should do:

▼ Declare to yourself and others that you will NOT give up, no matter what!

▼ Remember the children of Israel, who wandered for forty years before crossing over to Canaan. It does NOT matter how long you have been trying. The Promised Land lies ahead of you!

▼ Ask God to give you strength to know how to fight this battle. Be open to new "weapons" He might show you, such as a new food plan, exercise routine, or group to attend.

▼ Realize that your battle lies not only with an obsession with food, but also with Satan, who is "a liar and the father of lies" (John 8:44).

▼ Learn all you can about spiritual warfare and refuse to be defeated.

▼ Surrender the course of your battle to the Lord. Be patient. Encourage yourself in the Lord! (Psalm 42; 1 Samuel 30:6). You are in this for the long haul!

We do need a warrior's spirit to fight this battle. But because the prize is so great, the resistance from our enemy may be fierce too. Surrender to God, and this process, over and over.

I've often been asked why it takes so long to lose weight. "It's so SLOW!" everyone complains. Of course, experts tell us that losing weight slowly has physical benefits, such as we tend to lose more fat than muscle (which keeps our metabolism higher) and the toxins stored in fat are released at a more gradual pace.

But I think there are *spiritual* reasons that healthy weight loss is slow weight loss. Let's think about it this way. When you are a passenger and travel a long, complicated new route, what do you remember later? If I threw you the keys to the car and said, "Take us there again," would you be able to? If you were the driver, chances are you had to follow the map more closely. It slowed you down, but you probably learned the way well. And so you're not as likely to get lost or stray too far off-track.

Throughout your life, even if you successfully conquer the weight problem, your weight will fluctuate a bit. For women, it's normal to fluctuate a few pounds every month. And sometimes, especially around the holidays, it's easy to fluctuate too. If you haven't gone slowly along this path, you might panic and not remember how to find your way back. You might make some bad decisions and end up far off the LIFL road. The reality is that God is in control of your life and knows all about your walk through weight loss. And the journey will not be perfect, as you are not perfect. So keep your perspective—take heart and recognize that God wants you to succeed! And it's not about how fast you go anyway; it's about the fact that you keep going!

# THE BEST KEPT SECRET

You've learned how to invite God into this battle, and what you can expect Him to do for you, and why He says no to some of our weight loss prayers. We know He has mighty, wonderful plans for us, not only to help us shed excess weight, but to gain courage, hope, and discipline. God has the power to help you change unhealthy habits and embrace the new life He has created for you. And God loves you just the way—and weight—you are today. This is a God you can trust, because this is the God who loves you just as you are, and the God who believes you can become so much more.

*Lord, I can read these truths on a page, but until You put them in my heart, they can't really take hold in my life. Call to me every day, Lord, so that I will feel drawn to read Your Word and surrender my struggles to You. Help me accept the boundaries You've set for my appetite and my body. Give me the grace to say no to myself when I should. Give me the trust to hear Your affirmation of the unique plan for my life You've called me to and the unique beauty You've gifted me with. Amen.*

# seven

# LIVING THE LIFE

**Establishing New Behaviors into Lifelong Habits**

Congratulations! You've nearly finished this book, and you've made a big step towards losing the weight for life. You are now at the most critical stage of the weight loss journey. Here you will move from awareness and education to the act of making life-changing decisions. Yale researchers found that lasting weight loss occurs when a person takes control and puts into action what was learned as a new way of life. In fact, the researchers at Yale found that women who lose weight and keep it off successfully move through several distinct stages in the process.[1]

▼ You feel self-conscious but unaware of your own weight gain patterns.

▼ You recognize the problem and get educated.

▼ You take control and actively change your life.

**YOU ARE NOW AT THE MOST CRITICAL STAGE OF THE WEIGHT LOSS JOURNEY.**

Once you move into the taking control phase, you begin to experience positive reinforcement in increased self-confidence and self-esteem. That's why we're so proud of you: You've just moved from step one, to step two, and you're ready for the big leap into step three and your new life! Throughout the book, we've given you the tools you need to change your life, and change your weight. We've taught you what works, what doesn't, and helped you figure out a personal action plan that can carry you through to your goal. Now let's talk about how to stay on track until you reach your goal, and what to do once you're there.

## THREE SECRETS TO STAYING ON TRACK

Do yourself a favor . . . bookmark this page and review these three steps even as you lose weight, because they are great motivators. When you sense that you are falling short in any area, it's time to take action! You don't have to wait for the scale to register a gain.

### Self-Monitor

Self-monitoring means keeping tabs on your behavior and comparing it against what you know really works. For Lose

It For Life, it means following the basic guidelines you've learned:

▼ Eat when you are hungry, and stop when you are satisfied. Try to keep a food journal one day a week to monitor your intake.

▼ Make it a priority to get three servings of each food group, but most importantly, get in three daily servings each of dairy, fruits, and veggies. And don't forget to keep that water bottle handy.

▼ Get sixty minutes of movement in every day. If you aren't up to a workout just yet, commit to walking to get you in shape. You'll need to walk at least twenty minutes at a time, 3–6 days a week.

▼ Find an outlet for your emotions. Every day, reach out to a friend or spend time writing in your journal. Explore your feelings and understand the response they trigger.

▼ Practice building relationship skills so you'll have more peace and less to eat over.

▼ Spend time every day renewing your spirit and talking with God. Ask Him for the strength to change your habits, and make wise choices.

▼ Immerse yourself in this new life by creating relationships based on recovery, exploring new hobbies based on health and fitness, and giving yourself new goals to stay motivated.

You may be tempted once you've lost a significant amount of weight to stop self-monitoring, and to stop keeping track of your food intake. One benefit that we talked about in keeping a scorecard every day to track your servings of each food group is that you'll know right away when you're off track. Researchers who study obesity always complain that we underestimate how much we actually eat every day . . . but tracking keeps us rooted in reality. At the end of the day you see that you didn't polish off any veggies or fruits, but ate junk instead. You can start to make corrections right away, without losing time or gaining too much weight. It's easier to rebound from a bad day, than to rebound from a bad habit. Focus on small daily corrections and the bad habits won't get entrenched again.

One tip I've heard the pros say over and over is: Never regain more weight than you can lose in 2–3 days. That goal is realistic, but only if you're monitoring what you're eating, and weighing frequently. Which brings us to the most dreaded household appliance you'll ever own: the scale.

### Weigh Regularly

The folks in the National Weight Registry who lost weight and kept it off report weighing daily, or at least every week. Frequent checks like this mean you won't be surprised by a "sudden" 10-pound gain over Christmas. But for teens, who are already very focused on appearance and weight, weighing daily may increase the negative pressures you already feel. You'll have to use your best judgment on this one, but decide right now if you will weigh daily or once a week. Set a time and a place and keep it the same every time you weigh. It's normal to fluctuate a bit, especially around the time of your period, and especially if you're a young teen just before a growth spurt, so compare your weight to your scorecard on the All-These-In-3's meal plan (see page 177). If you're eating right and exercising, you don't have to panic when the scale moves a little higher than normal. Just keep doing what you've been doing and you will keep losing weight until your body reaches its ideal set point.

## QUICK TIPS

Studies show that successful weight loss maintenance is tied to incorporating more than one weight loss strategy into your daily routine.[2] Tricks to include:

▼ Automatically cut your entrée in half when served at a restaurant.

▼ Subscribe to a health or exercise magazine.

▼ Set new fitness goals regularly.

▼ Create a support group.

▼ Join Lose It For Life online.

### Keep Eating!

If your weight loss stalls, don't skip meals. Stay on the All-These-In-3's plan and increase your physical exercise. You may be tempted once you begin to experience control over your eating habits to restrict calories and cut meals. It's a tempting idea to think you can get skinnier and skinnier by eating less and less. But studies show that skipping meals actually leads to more overeating later on because of inconsistent meal patterns. Those who skipped meals were more likely to:

▼ rely on fast food

▼ get more of their calories from snacks and dinner

▼ drink more soft drinks[3]

Yikes! Skipping meals frequently and having inconsistent meal habits can really spell disaster for your healthy new lifestyle, no matter how much weight you've lost. So don't feel bashful about making mealtimes an important part of your routine. Eating breakfast, lunch, and dinner every day doesn't make you fat—it eliminates the temptations and traps other teens are falling into.

Eating a breakfast that has a source of lean protein (like an egg), a fruit or vegetable, and a whole-grain carbohydrate (1/2 a whole grain bagel, not a donut!) will help power-up your metabolism and burn fat. Your blood sugar will stay stable throughout the morning, and your performance at school might even improve!

## YOU MUST FIND THE COURAGE TO DO THE RIGHT THING FOR YOURSELF, EVERY DAY, NO MATTER WHAT.

I know it can be hard to give yourself permission to eat, especially in front of other people, if you have a lot of weight to lose. It's embarrassing to be overweight and hungry, especially when you're around someone who's thin and telling you all about how she never really eats. (Yeah, right.) You must find the courage to do the right thing for yourself, every day, no matter what. I would love to tell you it's going to be easy, but the reality is it's hard work. *But so worth it!* Expect to develop muscles in your body as well as muscles in your spirit. God will give you the strength to eat right and exercise, even when you feel self-conscious, if you will only ask Him. So keep moving and keep eating, and don't start skipping meals to "boost" your weight loss or cover embarrassment, because you'll actually slow weight loss down.

Sometimes living a new life is uncomfortable, especially during the early transitions. Trust us, you'll make mistakes! But there's a difference between accidentally eating past full one time and letting this become a habit which turns back into a lifestyle. To lose it for life, you'll need to be aware of the warning signs of a relapse.

## WHAT TO DO WHEN YOU BLOW IT

Everyone overeats at one time or another. Whether it's a national holiday like Thanksgiving, or just a great meal that was too delicious to stop eating, it can happen to anyone. So view it as part of the normal human experience . . . you're not abnormal if you blow it sometimes. You also shouldn't expect perfection from yourself on the All-These-In-3's meal plan.

But there is a difference between lean teens and over-weight teens in what they do after they overeat. Lean teens are more likely to compensate later in the day after they've eaten a big meal, by eating less. This finding is based on a study done by researchers at the Children's Hospital in Boston and the University of Minnesota. Both lean and overweight teens were given a super-sized fast food meal, and then asked to track their calories for the rest of the day. Overweight teens ate about 400 more calories than the lean teens by the end of the day. Lean teens had roughly the same daily caloric intake as any other day, despite the super-sized meal. Researchers noted that adjusting their caloric intake, as well as being more physically active, was a key reason why some teens stayed lean and some didn't. (Researchers also faulted the fast food industry's large portions for making it so easy to overeat.)

If you overdo it, eat less for the rest of the day and try to get more movement in. For instance, at dinnertime, add plenty of steamed veggies into the meal, and maybe add an extra walk after dinner too. Remind yourself to focus on smaller sizes, and listen for your body's "satisfied" signals when you are around tempting food. Forgive yourself and let it go. It's time to move on!

## THE FACE OF TOTAL RELAPSE

Overeating once or twice a year is "blowing it." But sometimes there is potential for a little accident to grow into a major disaster. The best offense here is good defense. You need to be aware of the signs of a total relapse to stop one from happening. If you see any of the following, or if people close to you have noticed, you are in danger of relapsing:[4]

▼ copping a rebellious attitude

▼ carrying negative feelings

▼ cutting yourself off from positive relationships

▼ complacency in exercising or going to support meetings

▼ confusion about "how I got here" and what really works

▼ compromising by exposing myself to situations that will cause me to fail

▼ compulsion to eat returns

Again, there's a difference between eating a bite or two more than you should have at lunch and eating out of fear or compulsion and being unable to stop. When you sense trouble is brewing and your old lifestyle is looking more and more comfortable, take positive steps to run from the relapse! Call a friend and make yourself accountable to them. Take yourself away from the problem area and pray that God would give you the strength to return to your established boundaries. Do not give up; instead, surrender again. Please, if you are struggling with what sounds like relapse, go to www.Loseitforlife.com and read the comments of others who have struggled with the same battle. You don't have to wage the battle alone.

One of my favorite anecdotes about the power of sin's lure is from Gordon MacDonald, a noted author and speaker. Gordon once reminded his audience that there are snakes which like to paralyze their prey first by sight and then by venom. If the little mouse stands still and looks at the snake, the snake can "charm" the mouse for the split second it needs to strike. If the mouse doesn't stop and look right into the eyes of the serpent, it has a chance to flee. We are like that mouse: If we don't stop and gaze into the eyes of our personal temptation, we can flee.

The twists of temptation can be fought if we heed God's call and escape from the activity our rebellious nature is pushing us toward. The best way to prevent a relapse is to not take that first destructive bite, to not give in to temptation.

*But encourage one another daily, as long as it is called Today,*
*so that none of you may be hardened by sin's deceitfulness.*

*We have come to share in Christ if we hold firmly till the end the confidence we had at first. As has just been said: "Today, if you hear his voice, do not harden your hearts."*

—HEBREWS 3:13–15

## STARTING A LIFL TEEN GROUP

A great motivator to stay on track (and out of the fridge!) is to build a community of support around you. Some of us have built up a protective wall of weight so we won't be hurt by people, but when we make the transition to letting the weight go and the people come near, we find they can actually *protect* us from unnecessary pain. God tells us: "Wounds from a friend can be trusted, but an enemy multiplies kisses" (Proverbs 27:6).

Friends can help nudge us along the slow and difficult path of restoration . . . and hope. Even when they have to confront us, they are helping us to heal and mature, and protecting us from spending a lifetime battling the same weary struggles we have already conquered. Our enemy, however, would have us incorrectly think being fat felt great all the time and watch in glee while we slipped further into depression and eating.

The Lose It For Life program has resources available to make that support a reality for you. First, you can establish your own Lose It For Life teen support group. By going online to LoseItForLife.com, you can download materials to begin a group and have regular meetings. You can have these groups in your home, at church, or anywhere you feel comfortable gathering together. Another option is to join our online support group. Not only do we have regular live chats with qualified counselors from the program, but we also have message boards that can help you connect with an online buddy. The team at Lose It For Life is always ready to support you, and we'd love to see you online! Joining an online program has some real advantages:

▼ According to a study published in the Journal of the American Medical Association, people who use online weight loss programs are more successful than those who try to lose weight alone.[5]

▼ In a recent year-long study of the effectiveness of Internet-based weight loss, people who spent more time on the study's weight loss site lost more weight than people who didn't spend time on the site.[6]

▼ After you drop the weight, an Internet-based program can help you maintain the weight loss as effectively as an in-person program.[7]

All of this boils down to complete immersion in a new lifestyle. By keeping in contact with others who are making the same changes, and renewing your mind each day with the spiritual, emotional, and educational resources that fuel lasting weight loss, there is success! As the major benefits of exercise are cumulative (which is why we have to exercise every day, not just once a year), the benefits of being in community add up, too, over the long run. So reach out, whether in person or online, and keep a steady stream of support coming your way.

## DON'T EVER GIVE UP!

The battle doesn't belong to the strong, but the persistent. No matter how many times you fall, keep getting up and trying again. Please don't ever let shame and despair stop you from moving in the right direction, be it only a little bit every day. Failing and falling are just part of this life, and they might slow you down, but they do not have to stop you. God doesn't judge or shame you, and neither do we at Lose It For Life. Failing is okay. Falling is okay. But *quitting* is not! So read this book (over and over if necessary!), find other resources online at LoseItForLife.com, and keep coming to the throne and asking for God's strength and mercy. He's given you these words to encourage you in the battle:

> Let us not become weary in doing good, for at the proper time we will reap a harvest if we do not give up.

—GALATIANS 6:9

Did you catch that? Sometimes all of our work seems to be yielding precious few results, and then, bam! We reap a harvest—if we haven't given up. The key to experiencing a bumper crop of rewards is to continue doing good, even when we're tempted to quit. Don't give up. There is a proper time for each of us to experience a harvest of overwhelming grace and overflowing blessings as we make the constant daily choice to do the right thing. God knows what He's doing. He knows where He's leading you. Don't get discouraged as you follow, especially when you stumble, because as long as you're facing the right direction, you're still making progress!

Some people say no one should plan for failure. We're telling you it's not popular or pleasant, but it could happen. So we don't plan to fail; we plan how to deal with stumbling so we can keep going. This is our prayer for you: that you would know some failures are inevitable, but that it's the total harvest that matters, not the individual seeds. Keep fighting the good fight, sister! We're praying for you, and you have the whole team at Lose It For Life on your side as well. You can do this, thanks to God's grace. And remember, you're not alone anymore!

~

*Lord, this book has opened my eyes to many areas of my life that need Your grace and power. Please open my ears to receive Your message into my life and my heart. It's not enough to know what the problem is now—I need Your strength to face it and continue my work through storms and droughts, exhaustion and frustration. I know there is a harvest for me, for us, to feast on and share with the needy world. May Your power and love bring it all to fruition at the proper time. Amen. I love You, God. I know You've heard me. Thanks.*

# Appendices

---

Food Diary

All-These-in-3's Scorecard

Prayer Journal

The Daily Tracker

# Appendix A

## Food Diary

**Date:**

| When I ate | What I ate | How much? | Was I Hungry? | Feelings |
|---|---|---|---|---|
| | | | | |
| | | | | |
| | | | | |
| | | | | |
| | | | | |
| | | | | |
| | | | | |
| | | | | |
| | | | | |
| | | | | |
| | | | | |
| | | | | |
| | | | | |
| | | | | |
| | | | | |
| | | | | |
| | | | | |
| | | | | |
| | | | | |
| | | | | |
| | | | | |

**Date:**

| When I ate | What I ate | How much? | Was I Hungry? | Feelings |
|---|---|---|---|---|
|  |  |  |  |  |
|  |  |  |  |  |
|  |  |  |  |  |
|  |  |  |  |  |
|  |  |  |  |  |
|  |  |  |  |  |
|  |  |  |  |  |
|  |  |  |  |  |
|  |  |  |  |  |
|  |  |  |  |  |
|  |  |  |  |  |
|  |  |  |  |  |
|  |  |  |  |  |
|  |  |  |  |  |
|  |  |  |  |  |
|  |  |  |  |  |
|  |  |  |  |  |
|  |  |  |  |  |
|  |  |  |  |  |
|  |  |  |  |  |
|  |  |  |  |  |

LOSE IT *for* LIFE *for* TEENS

**Date:**

| When I ate | What I ate | How much? | Was I Hungry? | Feelings |
|------------|------------|-----------|---------------|----------|
|            |            |           |               |          |
|            |            |           |               |          |
|            |            |           |               |          |
|            |            |           |               |          |
|            |            |           |               |          |
|            |            |           |               |          |
|            |            |           |               |          |
|            |            |           |               |          |
|            |            |           |               |          |
|            |            |           |               |          |
|            |            |           |               |          |
|            |            |           |               |          |
|            |            |           |               |          |
|            |            |           |               |          |
|            |            |           |               |          |
|            |            |           |               |          |
|            |            |           |               |          |
|            |            |           |               |          |
|            |            |           |               |          |
|            |            |           |               |          |

**Date:**

| When I ate | What I ate | How much? | Was I Hungry? | Feelings |
|---|---|---|---|---|
| | | | | |
| | | | | |
| | | | | |
| | | | | |
| | | | | |
| | | | | |
| | | | | |
| | | | | |
| | | | | |
| | | | | |
| | | | | |
| | | | | |
| | | | | |
| | | | | |
| | | | | |
| | | | | |
| | | | | |
| | | | | |
| | | | | |
| | | | | |
| | | | | |

**Date:**

| When I ate | What I ate | How much? | Was I Hungry? | Feelings |
|------------|-----------|-----------|---------------|----------|
|            |           |           |               |          |
|            |           |           |               |          |
|            |           |           |               |          |
|            |           |           |               |          |
|            |           |           |               |          |
|            |           |           |               |          |
|            |           |           |               |          |
|            |           |           |               |          |
|            |           |           |               |          |
|            |           |           |               |          |
|            |           |           |               |          |
|            |           |           |               |          |
|            |           |           |               |          |
|            |           |           |               |          |
|            |           |           |               |          |
|            |           |           |               |          |
|            |           |           |               |          |
|            |           |           |               |          |
|            |           |           |               |          |
|            |           |           |               |          |
|            |           |           |               |          |

# Appendix B

## The All-These-in-3's Scorecard

DAY _____

| Grains | Vegetables | Fruits | Milk | Protein | Fat |
|--------|-----------|--------|------|---------|-----|
| | | | | | |
| 3 | 3* | 3 | 3 | 3 | 3 |
|  |  |  |  |  |  |

DAY _____

| Grains | Vegetables | Fruits | Milk | Protein | Fat |
|--------|-----------|--------|------|---------|-----|
| | | | | | |
| 3 | 3* | 3 | 3 | 3 | 3 |
|  |  |  |  |  |  |

DAY _____

| Grains | Vegetables | Fruits | Milk | Protein | Fat |
|--------|-----------|--------|------|---------|-----|
| | | | | | |
| 3 | 3* | 3 | 3 | 3 | 3 |
|  |  |  |  |  |  |

DAY_____

| Grains | Vegetables | Fruits | Milk | Protein | Fat |
|--------|-----------|--------|------|---------|-----|
| | | | | | |
| 3 | 3* | 3 | 3 | 3 | 3 |
|  |  |  |  |  |  |

DAY_____

| Grains | Vegetables | Fruits | Milk | Protein | Fat |
|--------|-----------|--------|------|---------|-----|
| | | | | | |
| 3 | 3* | 3 | 3 | 3 | 3 |
|  |  |  |  |  |  |

DAY_____

| Grains | Vegetables | Fruits | Milk | Protein | Fat |
|--------|-----------|--------|------|---------|-----|
| | | | | | |
| 3 | 3* | 3 | 3 | 3 | 3 |
|  |  |  |  |  |  |

LOSE IT *for* LIFE *for* TEENS

DAY_____

| Grains | Vegetables | Fruits | Milk | Protein | Fat |
|--------|-----------|--------|------|---------|-----|
| | | | | | |
| 3 | 3* | 3 | 3 | 3 | 3 |
|  |  |  |  |  |  |

DAY_____

| Grains | Vegetables | Fruits | Milk | Protein | Fat |
|--------|-----------|--------|------|---------|-----|
| | | | | | |
| 3 | 3* | 3 | 3 | 3 | 3 |
|  |  |  |  |  |  |

DAY_____

| Grains | Vegetables | Fruits | Milk | Protein | Fat |
|--------|-----------|--------|------|---------|-----|
| | | | | | |
| 3 | 3* | 3 | 3 | 3 | 3 |
|  |  |  |  |  |  |

DAY _____

| Grains | Vegetables | Fruits | Milk | Protein | Fat |
|--------|-----------|--------|------|---------|-----|
| 3 | 3* | 3 | 3 | 3 | 3 |
|  |  |  |  |  |  |

DAY _____

| Grains | Vegetables | Fruits | Milk | Protein | Fat |
|--------|-----------|--------|------|---------|-----|
| 3 | 3* | 3 | 3 | 3 | 3 |
|  |  |  |  |  |  |

DAY _____

| Grains | Vegetables | Fruits | Milk | Protein | Fat |
|--------|-----------|--------|------|---------|-----|
| 3 | 3* | 3 | 3 | 3 | 3 |
|  |  |  |  |  |  |

DAY _____

| Grains | Vegetables | Fruits | Milk | Protein | Fat |
|--------|-----------|--------|------|---------|-----|
|        |           |        |      |         |     |
| 3      | 3*        | 3      | 3    | 3       | 3   |
|        |           |        |      |         |     |

DAY _____

| Grains | Vegetables | Fruits | Milk | Protein | Fat |
|--------|-----------|--------|------|---------|-----|
|        |           |        |      |         |     |
| 3      | 3*        | 3      | 3    | 3       | 3   |
|        |           |        |      |         |     |

DAY _____

| Grains | Vegetables | Fruits | Milk | Protein | Fat |
|--------|-----------|--------|------|---------|-----|
|        |           |        |      |         |     |
| 3      | 3*        | 3      | 3    | 3       | 3   |
|        |           |        |      |         |     |

DAY _____

| Grains | Vegetables | Fruits | Milk | Protein | Fat |
|--------|-----------|--------|------|---------|-----|
| | | | | | |
| 3 | 3* | 3 | 3 | 3 | 3 |
|   |   |   |   |   |   |

DAY _____

| Grains | Vegetables | Fruits | Milk | Protein | Fat |
|--------|-----------|--------|------|---------|-----|
| | | | | | |
| 3 | 3* | 3 | 3 | 3 | 3 |
|   |   |   |   |   |   |

DAY _____

| Grains | Vegetables | Fruits | Milk | Protein | Fat |
|--------|-----------|--------|------|---------|-----|
| | | | | | |
| 3 | 3* | 3 | 3 | 3 | 3 |
|   |   |   |   |   |   |

# Appendix C

## Prayer Journal

*God, thank You for:*

_____

_____

_____

_____

*I ask Your forgiveness for:*

_____

_____

_____

_____

*Please give me Your strength so I may:*

_____

_____

_____

_____

*And please do this for me also:*

_____

_____

_____

_____

# PRAYER JOURNAL

*God, thank You for:*

_____

_____

_____

_____

*I ask Your forgiveness for:*

_____

_____

_____

_____

*Please give me Your strength so I may:*

_____

_____

_____

_____

*And please do this for me also:*

_____

_____

_____

_____

# Prayer Journal

*God, thank You for:*

_____

_____

_____

_____

*I ask Your forgiveness for:*

_____

_____

_____

_____

*Please give me Your strength so I may:*

_____

_____

_____

_____

*And please do this for me also:*

_____

_____

_____

_____

God, thank You for:

_____

_____

_____

_____

I ask Your forgiveness for:

_____

_____

_____

_____

Please give me Your strength so I may:

_____

_____

_____

_____

And please do this for me also:

_____

_____

_____

_____

# THE DAILY TRACKER

There are five things you can do each day that will really keep you on track. That being said, keeping score isn't something you have to do. But if you are a list-type person, the DAILY Tracker may be just the tool to encourage you to bring the Lose It For Life principles all together as you begin your new lifestyle.

☐ **D**evotions?     Did I spend a few minutes either talking with God or reading His Word so I would be nourished and ready to surrender today?

☐ **A**ll-These-in-3's?     Did I make a good effort to stay on track with my eating today? Did I get enough water in?

☐ **I**ron woman?     How about exercise? I really needed sixty minutes today . . . did I get it in?

☐ **L**isten to me?     Did I spend a few minutes listening to what my heart and mind are telling me? What are my needs today? Did I talk with a friend about them or journal?

☐ **Y**es to my goals?     How was my relationship building today? What did I do that shows I'm immersing myself in my new life—including exploring new activities?

# 20 Insanely Easy Weight Loss Tips

1. *Substitute baby carrots for potato chips.* For every one baby carrot you swap out for one chip, you'll save about ten calories and one gram of fat. Make this substitute for twelve chips five days a week and you'll save 600 calories—which adds up to 9 pounds you'll lose within a year!

2. *Brush your teeth.* Successful weight loss gurus swear by this trick. Brushing your teeth after a meal seems to send a signal to your body that you're done eating. And it makes your breath fresh without relying on gum and mints made with sugar that can set you up to crave something sweet.

3. *Make the kitchen a "cooking and eating only" zone.* Don't do anything in the kitchen that isn't involved with eating. No homework, no talking on the phone, no painting nails at the table.

4. *Set the timer on snacks.* Limit your after-school grazing to 10 or 20 minutes, and brush your teeth when you're done. You'll send a signal to your appetite that you're done, and you can focus on something else. (Homework, anyone?)

5. *Put your fork down.* In between every bite, put down your fork or the food you're holding in your hands. Forcing yourself to separate bites like this will slow down your eating and help you recognize when you are full, which will help prevent overeating.

**6.** *Don't eat anywhere but at the kitchen table.* You'll pay more attention to what and how you're eating. Staying out of the kitchen except at meal times will reduce the chances of mindless grazing.

**7.** *Turn off the radio.* When a restaurant decides they want you "fed and out in forty minutes, they play music that pounds to 125 to 130 beats per minute— the faster the music, the faster you eat."[1] So either turn off the music or play slow, relaxing tunes that help you relax while you eat.

**8.** *Get some fresh air and sunshine.* "Too little sunlight can trigger cravings for high-calorie, fatty carbs like cakes, cookies, ice cream, and chips," says one weight loss expert.[2] Especially in the winter, get outside and get some fresh air and sunshine. Your body needs those rays to produce serotonin, a feel-good hormone in our brains that helps control cravings.

**9.** *Get a caffeine buzz.* Drinking an unsweetened, caffeinated cup of coffee or tea before a workout can help you burn more calories. In a recent study, "subjects who consumed at least 300 milligrams of caffeine two hours before a thirty-minute ride on a stationary bike burned a significantly greater number of calories than did their caffeine-free counterparts."[3] (Just don't take this as a license to drink the entire pot of coffee! A cup may help before a workout, but coffee-stained teeth aren't too appealing!)

**10.** *Don't get sweet on us.* The average person eats about a half pound of sugar every day![4] This epidemic of sugar-consumption may be related to the skyrocketing rates of obesity. Look for foods that have less than 5 milligrams of sugar per serving, and remember: The more sugar you eat, the more you'll want. The less sugar you eat, the better you'll feel.

11. *Drink like a fish, look like a gazelle.* Experts say drinking about eight glasses of water every day raises your metabolism slightly and allows your body to avoid retaining fluid. Drink a glass of water before every meal and before workouts.

12. *Avoid white starches.* Whole grains are great for weight loss, but refined white foods such as white bread, crackers, and donuts are proven to impact insulin levels which actually protects your stored fat instead of burning it.

13. *Don't stress out.* Stress can turn on your body's hormones that control fat storage, especially around your abdomen, and increase your appetite for carbohydrates.[5] To prevent stress from wreaking havoc with your diet, exercise every day, including taking short breaks throughout the day to climb the stairs or walk the dog. And keep plenty of fruits and vegetables around to snack on.

14. *Think small to lose big.* A study of dieters showed that those who focus on small goals such as losing only 5 to 10 percent of their body weight at a time were more successful at weight loss.[6] Small goals are not only easier to reach, but reaching them keeps your motivation high and your momentum building.

15. *Believe you can change.* In one study, women who worked on changing their thinking were the most successful at changing their weight.[7] To mimic their

success, remind yourself daily that only you can change your weight, one healthy choice at a time.

16. *Pack in protein power.* People who snack on protein stay full for up to forty minutes longer than those who don't.[8] For even more weight-loss power, include a complex carb with plenty of fiber, such as fruit and a lean dairy.

17. *Drink a glass of skim milk with every meal.* Eating dairy foods will help your body avoid storing fat and burn it instead. If the skim milk is replacing a sugar-sweetened soda or tea, you'll also be saving 150–300 calories a day . . . which can lead to a weight loss of 25 pounds within the year!

18. *Get plenty of sleep.* A study conducted at the University of Chicago Medical Center showed that lack of adequate sleep impairs your body's ability to process and store carbohydrates and also regulate hormones and blood sugar.[9]

19. *Skip the soda . . . and juice.* Women who drink sweetened soda and sweetened juice gain much more weight than women who drink one or less per month. Daily consumption of sweetened juices and soda are also linked to an increased risk of Type 2 diabetes.[10]

20. *Soup it up.* Research has shown that eating soup before a meal can reduce your caloric intake by up to 26 percent at the meal, and you won't "make up" for those calories later.[11] Great choices include broth-based soups and soups high in protein. Skip the cream soups because they contain more fat and calories.

# NOTES

## Chapter One

1. Xenical Orlistat home page, downloaded July 29, 2004.
2. "Statistics Related to Weight Control and Obesity," National Institutes of Health, http://www.niddk.nih.gov/health/nutrit/pubs/statobes.htm, retrieved September 8, 2004.
3. "Statistics Related to Weight Control and Obesity," National Institutes of Health, http://www.niddk.nih.gov/health/nutrit/pubs/statobes.htm, retrieved October 8, 2004.
4. "Defining Overweight and Obesity" Centers for Disease Control, http://www.cdc.gov/nccdphp/dnpa/obesity/defining.htm, retrieved September 8, 2004.
5. "A Day In the Life," Oct. 27, 2003, *ABCNews.com* abcnew.go.com/sections/Living/US/fatlikeme031027.html, downloaded on June 16, 2004.
6. "Fat Chance," *U.S News and World Report*, January 20, 2003, p.15.
7. "A Day In the Life," Oct. 27, 2003, *ABCNews.com* abcnew.go.com/sections/Living/US/fatlikeme031027.html, downloaded on June 16, 2004.
8. James M. Rippe, "The Role of Physical Activity in the Prevention and Management of Obesity," *Journal of the American Dietetic Association*, October 1998.
9. "Rising Obesity in Children Prompts Call to Action," *The New York Times*, August 26, 2003.
10. Nanci Hellmich, "Obesity Explodes From Teens to 20's," *USA Today*, October 13, 2003.
11. Steve Arterburn and Dr. Linda Mintle. *Lose It For Life*. Integrity, 2004.
12. Peg Tyre and Julie Scelfo, "Helping Kids Get Fit," *Newsweek*, September 22, 2003.
13. "Magazine Admits to Airbrushing Winslet," *BBC News World Edition*, Thursday, 9 January, 2003, 18:43 GMT, retrieved from bbc.co.uk/2/hi/entertainment/2643777.stm.

14. "Fitness Q & A's," American Council on Exercise, quoting Cedric X Bryant, 101 Frequently Asked Questions about "Health & Fitness" and "Nutrition & Weight Control." Sagamore Publishing, 1999.
15. Chart adapted with permission from Bray, G.A., Gray, D.S., Obesity, Part I, Pathogenesis, West J. Med. 1988: 149: 429–41.http://www.pueblo.gsa.gov/cic_text/health/setgoals/setgoals.htm.
16. Chart Adapted from "BMI for Age," Centers for Disease Control and Prevention, www.cdc.gov/growthcharts.
17. Adapted from "Setting Goals for Weight Loss," Federal Citizen's Information Center.

## Chapter 2

1. "Teen Dieting May Lead to Weight Gain," *Clinician Reviews*, February 2000.
2. Libby Tucker, "Diet Fact or Fiction?," *Science World*, January 12, 2004.
3. Label taken from http://vm.cfsan.fda.gov/~dms/foodlab.html.
4. Rebecca Gardy, "Teen Food Fetishes," *American Demographics*, March 1, 2003.
5. "Kids' Energy Needs Revised", USDA/ARS Children's Nutrition Research Letter at Baylor College of Medicine, retrieved online at http://www.bcm.edu/cnrc/consumer/nyc/vol1_03/vol1-03.htm.
6. Marianne McGinnis, "Weight Loss News: Snack on This," *Prevention*, February 2003, p.77.
7. Jessica Brown, "The 5 Nutrients You Need Now," *Diane, The Curves Magazine*, Spring 2004, p.38.
8. Gary Heavin, "The Exit Strategy From Dieting," *Diane, The Curves Magazine*, Spring 2004, p.60.
9. Maureen Callahan, M.S., R.D., "Low-Carb Lingo," *Health*, September 2004, p.154.
10. Marianne McGinnis, "Weight Loss News: Snack on This," *Prevention*, February 2003, p.77.
11. Anne Underwood and Jerry Adler, "What You Don't Know About Fat," *Newsweek*, August 23, 2004, p.42.
12. Ibid.
13. Adapted from Virtue, Doreen, "Constant Craving A-Z." (Carlsbad, CA: Hay House, 1999). Retrieved online May 10, 2004, from http://www.utexas.edu/student/cmhc/outreach/8traits.html.
14. Katherine Tallmadge, "15 Simple Tricks for Lasting Weight Loss," *Shape*, January 2003.
15. "Cinnamon Extracts Boost Insulin Sensitivity," *Agricultural Research Service*, July 2000.

16. Stacy Kennedy, M.P.H., R.D., L.D.N., C.N.S.D, "It's A Good Thing—Omega-3 Fats," *Intellihealth.com*, http://www.intelihealth.com/IH/ihtIH/WSIHW000/35320/35327/374556.html?d=dmtHMSContent, January 23, 2004.
17. Carol Simontacchi, "Is Our Diet Driving Us Crazy? Importance of a Balanced Diet for Good Brain Health," *Healthy & Natural Journal*, February 2001.
18. Salynn Boyles, "Drinking Water May Speed Weight Loss," *WebMD Medical News*, posted January 5, 2004 at http://content.health.msn.com/content/article/79/96070.htm?printing=true.
19. Dr. Steve Salvatore, "Calcium May Be Key to Taming Premenstrual Pain," *CNN.com Health* retrieved at http://www.cnn.com/HEALTH/9808/25/calcium.pms/, posted August 25, 1998.
20. Carol Krucoff, "Exercise & PMS," *iVillage Health*, http://www.ivillagehealth.com/conditions/reproductive/articles/0,,166043_125433-1,00.html.
21. Nancy Walsh, "Pelvic pain in teens is often nongynecologic—Diet may play a role," OB/GYN News, Sept.1, 2002.

*Chapter 3*

1. "Teen Taters, Too," *Science News*, April 26, 2003, Science Service, Inc.
2. "Born to Be Wired: Understanding the First Wired Generation" *Harris Interactive*, retrieved from http://us.i1.yimg.com/us.yimg.com/i/promo/btbw_2003/btbw_execsum.pdf.
3. Susan Smith Jones, Ph.D., "Metabolism Tune-Up," *Natural Beauty & Health*, retrieved online 8/17/04 at Http://www.nbhonline.com/articles/Health./metabolism.html.
4. Christine Hurley Deriso, "Study Cites Benefits of Exercise for Teens," Medical College of Georgia press release, July 6, 2004.
5. "Short Bouts of Exercise Help Adherence" American Running Association, retrieved from http://www.americanrunning.org/displayindustryarticle.cfm?articlenbr=2380 on October 16, 2004.
6. John P. Foreyt, "The role of behavioral counselor in obesity treatment," *Journal of the American Dietetic Association*, October, 1998.
7. Gary Heavin, "The Exit Strategy From Dieting," *Diane, The Curves Magazine*, Spring 2004, p.60.
8. James M. Rippe, "The Role of Physical Activity in the Prevention and Management of Obesity," *Journal of the American Dietetic Association*, October 1998.
9. Ibid.
10. Ibid.

11. Jack H. Wilmore, "Exercise, obesity, and weight control," Originally published as Series 1, Number 6, of the PCPFS *Research Digest*, retrieved online at http://www.fitness.gov/activity/activity7/obesity/obesity.html.

12. Martin Padgett Jr., "Instant Gratification: Nine Ways Exercise Helps Right Away," *ABC News.com*, posted February 14, 2001, at http://abcnews.go.com/sections/living/MensHealth/menshealth_1.html.

13. "Exercise Improves Learning and Memory," *Howard Hughes Medical Institute*, posted November 9, 1999, at www.nnmi.org//news/sejnowski.html.

14. Ibid.

15. Kathy Stevens, "Interval Training: Alternating Periods of High and Low Intensity Exercise for Maximum Benefit," *American Fitness*, July–August 1997.

16. Borg RPE scale, © Gunnar Borg, 1970, 1985, 1994, 1998.

17. "Sweat Off Stress," *Prevention*, February 2003.

## Chapter 4

1. Stephen Arterburn, "A Flashpoint Moment That Changed Everything," posted December 11, 2002, at www.LoseItForLife.com.

2. Maria Noel Mandile, "Using Your Mind To Lose Weight," *Natural Health*, April 2002.

3. Questions adapted from Mintle, L. (2002). *Breaking Free from Compulsive Overeating*. Lake Mary, Florida: Charisma House.

4. Maria Noel Mandile, "Using Your Mind To Lose Weight," *Natural Health*, April 2002.

5. R.M. Ganley, "Review: Emotions and Eating in Obesity," *Nutrition Research Newsletter*, June 1989.

6. Marilyn Elias, "Moms Often Unaware That Kids Are Overweight," *USA Today*, May 5, 2003.

7. Adapted from Mintle, Dr. Linda and Steve Arterburn, *Lose It For Life*, Integrity, 2004.

8. Dr. Jill Hubbard, "Anxiety and Coping with Our Fears," posted July 18, 2003, at www.LoseItForLife.com.

9. "The New Plague? Obese Kids Have Adult-Sized Health Problems," *ABCnews.com*, January 24, 2004, retrieved at http://abcnews.go.com/sections/2020/DailyNews/2020_obesekids030124.html.

10. Cheryl Graybill, MA, MFT, "Just Feel It!" posted to *LoseItForLife.com*, September 29, 2003.

11. Dr. Linda Mintle and Stephen Arterburn, *Lose It For Life*, Integrity, 2004.

12. Geneen Roth, "Love, Loss, and What I Ate," *Prevention,* June 2004.

## Chapter 5

1. Lee Dye, "Vital Connections: Study Finds Friendship Problems Are Bigger Factor for Suicidal Girls," *ABCNews.com,* posted January 29, 2004, at http://abcnews.go.com/sections/SciTech/DyeHard/suicide_girls_dyehard_040129.html.
2. Susan Eppley, Ed.D, "Self Talk," posted on February 23, 2004, to LoseItForLife.com
3. "Media and Girls," *Media Awareness Network,* retrieved online on 8/21/04 at www.media-awareness.ca/english/issues/stereo-typing/women_and_girls/women_girls.cfm?
4. "Success Stories: National Study Finds Winning Weight Loss Strategies," *ABCNews.com,* posted June 2, 2004, at http://ABCnews.go.com/sections/GMA/DrJohnson/Diet_registry_040602.html.
5. Kathleen Doheny, "Weight Loss Support Systems-LifeHealthy News," *Shape,* March, 2004.
6. "Certain Behaviors Can Predict Binge-Eating Disorders In Teenage Girls," *Center for the Advancement of Health,* March 14, 2002.
7. "Dianne Neumark-Sztainer, Ph.D., Mary Story, Ph.D., Peter J. Hannan, Mstate, Terri Tharp, MPH, Jeanna Rex, MEd, "Factors Associated With Changes in Physical Activity: A Cohort Study of Inactive Adolescent Girls," *Pediatrics & Adolescent Medicine,* Vol. 157 No. 8, August 2003.
8. Michelle J. Pearce, Julie Boergers, Mitchell J. Prinstein, "Adolescent Obesity, Overt and Relational Peer Victimization, and Romantic Relationships," *Obesity Research,* 10:386–393, 2002.
9. "Sex and relationships in the Media," *Media Awareness Network,* retrieved 8/21/2004 from http://www.media-awareness.ca/english/issues/stereotyping/women_and_girls/women_sex.cfm
10. "Adolescent Obesity and Romantic Relationships," *Nutrition Research Letter,* June, 2002.

## Chapter 6

1. "Vital Stats," *Health,* January/February 2003.
2. Jennifer Cecil, M.Ed., CPC, *"Weight loss and the Warrior Spirit,"* retrieved 7/26/2004 from www.LoseItForLife.com.

## Chapter 7

1. "Yale Researchers Find Pattern In Maintaining Weight Loss," *Nursing Science Quarterly,* Vol. 17:pp 242–252.

2. "Does Weight Loss Maintenance Become Easier Over Time?" *Nutrition Research Newsletter,* October 2000.

3. Anna Maria Siega-Riz, "U.S. Teens and the Nutrient Contribution and Differences of Their Selected Meal Patterns," *Family Economics and Nutrition Review,* Winter 2001.

4. Steve Arterburn, "Seven Keys/Preservation," retrieved from www.LoseItForLife.com.

5. Maria Noel Mandile, "Use Your Mind to Lose Weight," *Natural Health,* April 2002.

6. "Internet Weight Loss Program Effective Among Adults at Risk for Diabetes," *Brown University News Service,* Distributed April 8, 2003.

7. Kathleen Doheny, "Weight Loss Support Systems," *Shape,* March, 2004.

## Appendix E

1. Carol Krucoff, "Is Your House Making You Fat?" *Prevention,* downloaded 9/12/04 at http://www.prevention.com/cda/feature2002/0,2479,sl-6269,00.html.

2. Robin Vitetta-Miller, "Beat Winter Weight Gain!," *Shape,* November 2003.

3. Dan Gordon, "Goodbye, Fat Body!," *Men's Fitness,* December 2003.

4. Laura Casanova, "Our Growing Children," *HealthSmart Today,* Fall 2004.

5. Kelly James Enger, "Is Stress Making You Fat?" *Vibrant Life,* July–August 2003.

6. Alice Lesch Kelly, "The Secret Strategies for Lasting Weight Loss," *Shape,* March 2002.

7. Ibid.

8. Marianne McGinnis, "Snack on This," *Prevention,* downloaded November 8, 2004 at prevention.com.

9. "Lack of Sleep Alters Hormones, Metabolism, Simulates Effects of Aging," The University of Chicago Hospitals, October 21, 1999.

10. Rob Stein, "A Regular Soda a Day Boosts Weight Gain," *The Washington Post,* Wednesday, August 25, 2004; Page A01.

11. Matthew Rodgers, "Foods That Fight Fat," *Woman's Day,* downloaded November 8, 2004, at womansday.com.